BARBEQUE'N WITH BOBBY

by Bobby Seale

Ten Speed Press

1☉
Ten Speed Press
P. O. Box 7123
Berkeley, CA 94707

Book design, typography, and cover design by
Fifth Street Design Associates, Berkeley, CA
Cover photo by Steven M. Falk
Illustrations by Ife Nii Owoo

Library of Congress Catalog Number: 88-050002
ISBN 0-89815-242-9 (paper)
ISBN 0-89815-243-7 (cloth)

First Printing, 1988

Printed in the United States of America

1 2 3 4 5 6 — 93 92 91 90 89 88

CONTENTS

DEDICATION

IN MY FAMILY, BARBEQUE'N IS A DOWN-HOME family tradition. At those festive gatherings the children, whose finicky palates seem to be conditioned to dislike most foods, savor and enjoy barbeque. With this reminiscence, my wife Leslie Seale and I, dedicate this book to the children of our immediate family: To my two sons, Malik Nkrumah (named after Malcolm X and Kwamie Nkrumah) and Romaine Fitzgerald (after a former Black Panther who, at this writing, is still a political prisoner); to my three nieces, Charlotte Yvonne Williams (my sister's daughter), Mercelle Yvonne Seale and Abraxas Kai Seale, (my brother's daughters); and to my brother-in-law's children: Shanta, Danta, Shela, Tonya, Bryant, Toni and Dewey Johnson, Jr. III. I further dedicate this book to the person who has always told me, "Daddy, you make the best barbeque in the world"; my youngest child and namesake, my daughter, J'aime *Bobbie* Seale.

ACKNOWLEDGEMENTS

THERE ARE SO MANY FAMILY MEMBERS AND FRIENDS who deserve acknowledgement. A book of this type can only be produced after years of recipe trial and error, and praises from those who have tried, tasted, savored and enjoyed my barbeque'n methodology which has literally taken generations to perfect. With this in mind, I begin my acknowledgements by praising my deceased uncle, Tom Turner, who kept the 'secret' baste-marinade method alive by teaching it to me. A special praise to my parents Thelma and George Seale. Mama, for raising my brother, sister, and me to be self-sufficient (teaching us to cook many of our own meals), and to "share and share alike . . . and to do unto others as we would have them do unto us." George (we always called our father George), for teaching me carpentry and by taking me fishing and hunting at a young age (barbequed big and small game was always a treat!). To my sister Bettye (Seale) Williams, who led part of the way when we were teenagers for my creative cooking methods. To my brother John and his wife Sandra who put up with my grandiose barbeque video-production experimentations in their beautifully modernized (and ultra clean) kitchen and neat backyard when I first began to write this book in 1982.

I want to give *tribute* to all the former Black Panther Party members, (and all the community workers of the B.P.P.) who, during the 1960s protest era, fed the needy, helped register people to vote, preserved the health of the people, many times putting their lives on the line, and protected and loved the community. Those invincible brothers and sisters were dedicated beyond words and gladly volunteered and worked hard with a socially responsible involvement on many programs and multi-thousand plate barbeque fund-raisers (you haven't barbequed until you've prepared righteous, down-home barbeque for 5,000 people! . . . all of whom maintained they savored every bite). It was a time when many Black Panther Party central committee meetings had to be held in the headquarter's office kitchen. Why? Because many times, as chairman and key organizer I would happen to be smothering some meat or stewing a gigantic vat of my hickory chili to feed the daily hard-working party members. Without the powerful memories of those community-organizing days, and especially the fund-raising barbeque events, I honestly believe I would not have considered the idea of writing this book.

To Jerry Rubin, who was really the first to enthusiastically suggest that I write a cookbook. While we were both political prisoners in 1969 during the Great Chicago 8 Conspiracy Trial, I would go on and on, describing recipes detail by detail on how I would prepare my favorite dishes (jail food was horrendous . . . and with other prisoners we would rap many times about what I could cook or barbeque and what we would eat if we were out). To my friends and past co-defendants Abbie Hoffman, Tom Hayden, John Forones, Renie Davis and especially Lee Weiner and Dave Dillinger for all their years of encouragement and support since the trial. And also William Kunstler, Leonard Wineglass, and Charles Garry, our attorneys. To Elliott Gould, Peter Boyle, and particularly Carl Lumbly (who played me), all the other actors, and Jeremy Kagan, the director and writer of the HBO movie special *Conspiracy: The Trial of the Chicago 8*, all who encouraged me when they heard that I was writing this book.

A special thanks for all the encouragement and support from Peter Liacouras, President of Temple University; Eldridge Smith, Director of Admissions; George Ingram, University News Bureau Director; and Lois S. Cronholm, Dean of the College of Arts and Sciences. And many thanks to Temple University's Dr. Jayne Kribbs and other Associate Deans and all the staff of the College of Arts and Sciences and several hundred Temple University faculty, staff, and students who have expressed their support and "savory" encouragement for me to hurry up and get my book finished.

To Dr. Molefi K. Asante, chairman of the Department of African-American Studies of Temple University who has enthusiastically encouraged and supported the publication of this book. I further acknowledge him for his support of the many ideas I've expressed on how to use this book to assist many grassroots community organizations, and the development of the Bobby Seale Scholastic Awards Fund, and to Benita Brown and all the faculty and staff of the Department of African-American Studies (AAS) for their direct and indirect help and "savory" support, and to AAS Associate Professor, Dr. Sonja Peterson-Lewis for her enthusiastic conversational input which helped me to finalize my comedic but serious culinary idea of the "Barbeque Bill of Rights." To Muriel Feelings, Temple University Director of the Pan-American Studies Community Education Program (PASCEP), whose Roots Night Program featured my barbeque delights with the final completion of this book.

Special acknowledgements to William "Bill the Hunter" Morris, a barbeque "technologist," who made it his "friendship" business to get my barbeque method down to a T, and his wife Karen, for the use of their home, kitchen and mini-community park they developed, and for the photographs of barbeque events and help in times of need. I want to thank Bill Morris, Michael Scott, Bill "The Fireman" Moseley, and many others for all their help in pit-quing coordinated barbeque events while this book was in its final stages.

To Ahada Stanford for all her friendship and financial support in times of need, for the use of her home for barbeque events, and especially for the many brain-storming sessions we have had related to my many projects, and the completion and marketing of this book.

To Bill Chestnut, who has savored every bite, Joe Northern, a master chef in his own right, and William "Sonny" Hayes, owner of "Sonny's Knife and Fork'" restaurant, all who have encouraged, admired and supported the efforts behind this book and other projects. And in this same category, Norman Brooks, who states unequivocally, "No Way! If you try to out-barbeque Bobby Seale in a contest, you lost from jump street." And to hear Norman argue on, "Naw, I don't want to hear nothing about no *secret* recipe. Bobby will give you *his* recipe. Any one you want. You can use it or just know what he does, and he'll still barbeque—No! He'll *bobby-que* circles around you. No contest. Forget it!"

To Natalie Mitchell, our manager at Cafe Society, and a "co-cooking" friend of mine who added my goober ingredients to one of her recipe side dishes. Her Goobered Sweet Potatoe Pie made a hit at the Philadelphia Mayor's 1984 "Cook and the Book" event held at Judy Wicks' "White Dog Cafe." And to Judy Wicks herself who literally loved the idea of this "one and only" down-home hickory-smoked barbeque cooking guide.

Jae DuBois, for all of her weekly *Cafe Society* Sunday morning supportive conversational perceptions related to the refinement and completion of this book. To Marie Myers for her very friendly barbeque rib-eating "savory" support and the same acknowledgement to all the many friends and acquaintances at Philadelphia's Cafe Society who cheered me on, whose names and nicknames are too many to mention here, but here are a momentous, gregarious few: James "Pat" C. Patterson, Tyric Armstead, Laura Shields, Michael Scott, Roland Kemp and his brother, Leon, and Bonita Grant, Mr. Chew, Vennie Boswell, Ramona Flippen, Mr. Skip, Michael "Cutty" T. Cutner, Carl Slater and Charles "Valdez" Slater, Frenchy, Veneta Despot, Louise the lively barmaid, Lenwood, Creg, Joe Evans, Little Marie, Harvey Brownstine, Bob Wallace, Dough, John Groves, former Philadelphia Policeman and community friend, Marion Rogers, Malcolm "Butch" Thomas, Stan the Man, Darell Wescot, Augustus "Gus" Patterson, "Doc" Reddman, Randy Alexander, Earnest Jackson, Pamela Moss and Greg Bell. Oh! Eddie English, Eddie Evans, Cafe Society's comedic "expert" Ira T. Watts the 3rd, and his father Ira T. Watts the 2nd, Rufus Haggard, Marie and her daughter Stephanie Robinson, and all the other friends and acquaintances who have tried, tasted, savored and enjoyed my barbeque'n methodology.

To Denise Black and Eloise West who assisted me in the final months of retyping, editing and numerous weekend coordinating efforts which helped to structure this book and whose assistance and enthusiastic support (during many late hours) were undaunted until the work was completed.

To Arlene Jones-Smith and her husband Roosevelt Smith who typed the first three drafts of this book at a time when I was not even sure of the correct cookbook language to use, and my good friend Regina Jennings, the creative writer who helped edit and structure the initial material for this book.

To Carol Henderson, cookbook editor, and George Young, Ten Speed Press managing editor whose sharp eyes and perspectives helped me finish this work, and to Jo Ann Deck whose hours of valuable time and patience helped me complete this book.

To my mother-in-law, Elizabeth E. Johnson, who has always stood behind me in this and many other efforts and without whose loving support and without whose house, kitchen, backyard and electric lights in the early morning hours, I would not have been able to complete this book.

To Dewey Johnson, my brother-in-law, whose crazy joke-filled antics always made our barbeque occasions a joyful *happening*! To a few of our family cousins who ate and praised many *final* (for recipe writing) cookout barbeque meals: George Burrows, Diane and her family, and Richard, Mikey, and Ann Harding, and especially Elaine (Ivory) Harding, the professional model in our family who would pig-out on many occasions from Denver to Philadelphia, not being able to resist my mouth-watering barbeque treats.

And last but certainly not least, to Leslie, my wife, whose love, admiration and wholehearted support with numerous weekend initial barbeque recipe-note cookouts have made the writing of this book possible . . . . "Bobby," she would say, "you can't say a little bit of this and a dash of that . . . . I know what you mean, but will the reader?"

To everyone of the above and many others, I acknowledge and thank them. I thank them in the spirit, realization, and principles of cooperational humanism.

BOBBYQUE? YES!

THERE IS A DISTINCT CONNECTION BETWEEN the spelling or the pronunciation of a word and its cultural etymological root — that is, the true meaning of what people do culturally and how they refer to it. When I first began to write this barbeque cookbook, I felt the strongest urge to look up *barbeque* in the dictionary. To my surprise my spelling didn't appear before me. I found my treasured word but with the spelling *barbecue* — meaning to roast or broil on a rack over hot coals or over a revolving spit before or over a source of cooking heat. Historically, the word was pronounced "ba ba coa" by the Taino people of the Bahamas.

Oddly enough, throughout all my years from Texas to California, I had very seldom seen a pit or restaurant sign that used the dictionary spelling *barbecue* (especially in the Black community). When I had seen such signs near or outside my community, I didn't feel that familiar mouth-watering effect which my favorite food could provoke instantly. I later began to think perhaps I had an inborn prejudice to such signs because in the Black community the word was always spelled "Bar Be *Que*" or "Bar B Que" or initialed "B B Q," and accompanied with that special hickory aroma. I began to feel that the "*cue*" spelling represented something drab, or even "square," as we used to say in the 1950s. My realization was that most restaurants whose signs lacked the suffix -que seemed to be void of that ever-pervasive down-home hickory-smoked aroma which would literally carry for blocks.

If the hickory-smoked aroma carried for blocks, surely the word of mouth praises carried for miles. My Uncle Tom Turner's Bar B Que Pit restaurant in Liberty, Texas, had just such a reputation. It was said that people would come from as far as one hundred miles just to feast on his barbeque delights.

I can remember clearly in 1950 the first two weeks of my Texas vacation in the late summer through early fall. My parents had moved from Texas to California following wartime job opportunities in the midforties, but late summers were reserved for going back to our roots. My parents missed Texas and would faithfully return to visit our kinfolk and loved ones throughout southeastern Texas — Jasper County, Beaumont, and Liberty.

Soon after arriving in Texas, our summer-fall vacations were often highlighted by attending huge church association fanfares. Under enormous tents which sheltered us from the blazing Texas sun, we'd feast on dishes prepared by the sisters of the church. Sweet potato pie, fried chicken and fish, and barbeques of smoked beef and spareribs were prepared by the men and women at the pits. In the midst of happy greetings, praises to the Lord, and harmless gossip, I'd hear statements like: "This *bobbyque* sho' is good! But Lawd, it takes Tom Turner to really bobbyque some meat!"

Bobbyque? Yes! To my young ears it always sounded like that, an idiomatic expression I certainly didn't question. For most of my life, when black folks pronounced *barbeque*, the first two syllables literally sounded like my name.

One year my favorite first cousin Alvin was leaving for the remainder of the vacation to spend time with his father, Tom Turner. I remember tearfully convincing my mama to let me go, too. I wanted to be near the soulful restaurant activity and luscious presence of the hickory-smoked food I couldn't get enough of. When we arrived, Uncle Tom greeted Alvin and me in his southern Texas hospitable style. He said we could eat to our fill plus earn two dollars a day if we would help him around his barbeque restaurant. Through the first week, I watched Uncle Tom with wide-eyed innocence as he went about the daily chores of preparing barbeque from early morning pit fire to afternoon scrumptious delights.

Because of my daily interest, Uncle Tom guided me through his secret process, teaching me how to place the hickory wood, burn it down, and spread the coals. He explained the importance of having a pit fire without any flames. He would pull out slab after slab of sizzling ribs, whole chickens, and browning hunks of roast beef and dip them into a large metal washtub of what he called "base." I could hear the watery drippings of the "base" sting as the droplets hit the hot hickory wood coals. The smoke conjured up a potion that would make me heady, almost paralyzed by its appetizing aroma.

"Bobbyque smells good, huh, Bobby?" said Uncle Tom smiling one day.

"Uncle Tom, it's the *best* in the world!" I exclaimed.

"How you know?" laughed Uncle Tom.

"I done ate some of everybody's bobbyque . . . . Out in California and all over Texas . . . . And yo's is da best!"

Uncle Tom laughed as he hustled a hunk of browning beef out of the pit and dunked it once again into the washtub of baste. He would dip or mop-baste thirty or forty slabs of spareribs in the pit, turn them, and baste them again, and again.

"When you make bobbyque, you don't put no sauce on it till it's done. Da base makes it tenda. Taste good right down to da bone," Uncle Tom would say matter-of-factly. The "base" marinade was the key. It was Uncle Tom's secret method: onions, peppers, garlic, lemon juice, vinegar, celery, and seasonings placed in two large boiling pots of water. "We gotta let dease ribs soak in da base ova night," Uncle Tom would say as he poured "base" over the meats placed in the washtubs.

The meats were marinated before the pit-smoking, then constantly dipped in or mopbasted with the marinade throughout the pit-smoking process. That delicious taste was further accentuated by the steaming smoke of the hickory wood in a large enclosed brick pit. This process was the secret behind that fascinating aroma and taste.

Throughout my month-long vacation I absorbed Uncle Tom's culinary art while I dreamed of owning such a restaurant some day. I happily served customers, many times watching them savor the moment and hearing their praises and compliments. My vacation was ending too soon. However, since I'd been such a good worker and pupil, Uncle Tom let me prepare a small batch of barbeque before I left for California. After I finished, I chose the juiciest slab of ribs and hunk of beef, and presented them to Uncle Tom for his opinion. "Bobby, boy, dis' heah is some really good bobbyque!" Elated by the compliment, I hopped around the restaurant with a feeling of youthful accomplishment and my twelve-year-old chest poked out. It was a time I've never forgotten. I had been given the chance and the secret recipe method to prepare the food I loved the most. I decided that from that day on I would prepare barbeque like Uncle Tom "qued" it for the rest of my life. However, when I returned home to California, little did I realize that it would be years before I focused on the idiomatic expression, "bobbyque" and its etymology, and why it was pronounced like my name.

After a four-year stint in the U.S. Air Force, and a couple of years as a comedian and jazz drummer, I enrolled at Merritt College in Oakland, California. The third semester I chose cultural anthropology as an extracurricular course. With the advent of the 1960s there grew a burning desire among my college peers and myself to know about Black American and African history. Reading Jomo Kenyatta's *Facing Mount Kenya* I had the fantastic realization that Tarzan did not run Africa, and I wanted to know about my African ancestors who did. Following up a footnote, I encountered an article alluding to the roots of surviving Africanisms in Afro-American English. Black English? Throughout my early school years I had often been criticized for pronouncing words incorrectly. My black and white teachers alike would vehemently criticize and say I spoke "pigeon language" or broken English. For example I would say "dese" instead of "these"; "flo" instead of "floor"; "do," pronounced *doe*, instead of "door," etc.

Preparing a term paper for my cultural anthropology class, I chose the subject of West African agricultural sites — that is, what particular vegetables, fruits, and other plants were first cultivated by African Homo sapiens. It was an unconscious choice even though the topic was connected with food. Reading through a book entitled *Myth of the Negro Past*, by Melville J. Herskovits, I followed up another footnote that made reference to a Black professor of English, Dr. Lorenzo Dow Turner. Dr. Turner had published *Africanisms in the Gullah Dialect* (1949), a work on his twelve years of field expeditions researching surviving Africanisms in Black American language via West African ethnic groups and South American and Caribbean descendants of West Africans. It was yet another fantastic realization to find out that certain idiomatic expressions had survived among Black folks in the United States. There was a distinct reason why Blacks in the U.S. and elsewhere in the Americas pronounced many English words as they did.

Dr. Turner also pinpointed a number of surviving words from Africa in the U.S., some of which related to food and plants first developed and cultivated in West Africa. From an anthropological standpoint, the stringy yam arguably comes from the Senegalese area, the location of Alex Haley's *Roots*. *Yam* originally meant "to eat." Kola nuts, a main ingredient in Coca Cola and other cola beverages, were first cultivated in West Africa. While "kola" sounds African, the English word *cola* is not an African word. *Goober* as in Granny Goose's Goobers (packaged peanuts) or the candy bar Goobers, is a direct surviving African word from the Congo and Angola areas. *Goober* derives from *nguba* and *gooba* (without the "er" or rolling "r" pronunciation), a word that means "nuts" that one eats. My research also revealed that watermelon, cotton, and okra were first cultivated in West Africa. The African Bantu word for okra is *gumbo*. This word has survived because of African-American and Louisiana Creole usage. Gumbo is a very popular fish and shellfish southern stew which contains okra.

Dr. Turner's intent was also to prove that Black American idiomatic expressions had little to do with our White American southern drawls or dialects. After twelve years of field research (six in West Africa, six in South America and the Caribbean), Dr. Turner found that certain idiomatic inflections reflected surviving Africanisms in Black American language which contribute to how blacks pronounce many words.

Many Black Americans pronounce such words as *these* "dese," *those* "dose," *floor* "flo" and *barbeque* "bobbyque." Here the lack of the "ar" sound produced "bobby" instead of "barbe." The "th," "er," and "ar" sounds are in fact absent in West African language, and Black Americans are largely descendants of West African peoples. The etymological path has been "ba ba coa," barbacoa, barbe*cue*, *barbe*que, and "bobbyque."

No one knows exactly what the "ba ba coa" meant historically and culturally to the Taino and West Indian peoples. However, whether you are a New World African-American, Euro-American, Asian-American, or Native American, the present-day American barbeque is an exciting and culturally appetizing event. Everything about the word barbe*que* (or bobbyque!) evokes pleasure. To *que* the meat to that special flavor–to *que* the meat to a luscious hickory-smoked tenderness — to *que* it with my traditional down-home recipe-method, will "que" a person's heart, mind, and soul to expect a delectable experience, thanks to barbeque secrets handed down to me by my Uncle Tom Turner and passed on to you in this book.

Righteous down-home barbeque has been developed all over America with considerable improvisation. Perfection can only come from trial and error over many years. Thousands of culinary experts, particularly in the South, guard and hoard their secret recipes and methods. I happen not to be one of those people.

Having traveled extensively across the United States (over 40 states several times over), I have tasted some of the best and the worst barbeque prepared around the country. At the 1987 fifth annual "twenty-five thousand dollar first prize" National Rib Cook-Off, in Cleveland, Ohio, I was selected to be one of the judges of the contest for the "Best Ribs in America." For two whole days I had the opportunity to eat and evaluate barbeque ribs from Hawaii and all corners of the U.S., and from countries around the world: Mexico, Canada, Australia, England, Hong Kong, and Ireland. Barbequing in all its contemporary activity, recipes, and methods has truly become an international festive occasion, a culinary example of human creativity.

From years of testing and tasting, with my Uncle Tom's recipe-methods as my starting point, I've developed my own contemporary southern-style, hickory-smoked barbeque recipes that have delighted the taste buds and appetites of politicians, writers, community activists, movie stars, family and friends, and thousands more at numerous barbeque fundraisers. For over thirty-five years I have perfected my pit-fire techniques, my sauces and bastes, so that they will be distinguished from the commercial and many times bland recipes found on "bottle-backs"

With its wide variety of hickory-smoked meats, fish, and poultry entrees and its baste-marinades and barbeque sauces, you can't miss with this book. Also included are many delicious southern-style side dishes such as Hickory Honey-Seasoned Collard Greens, Hickory-Hocked Black-Eyed Peas, Marshmallow-Orange Pit-Baked Sweet Potatoes, and Bacon-Cheddar Southern Corn Bread. At the end are recipes for salt free, low sodium and sugarless barbeque entrees and accompaniments. I'm sure this book will answer many questions you may have had about preparing and getting the best results from backyard pit-grill, smoke barbequing. With this work I've outlined my creative recipe-methods on how to "do it" like Bobby Seale and my Uncle Tom would "que" it.

Barbequing doesn't have to be an isolated festive occasion set aside only for holidays and summer days. With this book, the American tradition of barbequing can become your own savory, mouthwatering regular dining event. On the other hand, barbequing can also be the attraction or fund-raising occasion for your social or community event.

With more than one hundred recipes, this work becomes part of a continuing culinary contribution to the American and intercommunal world-wide culture. If you "bobby-que" with me and creatively improvise with me, or just follow my recipes to a T, I guarantee that you will spice up your lifestyle and add the very best contemporary down-home barbeque cuisine to your culinary endeavors. So with these mouth-watering recipes I invite you to participate in barbequing, or, if you will, "bobby-que'n" — a truly American act of soulful hospitality.

Bobby Seale
United States of America.

MY CONTEMPORARY HICKORY QUEST

HICKORY, FRUIT, AND MESQUITE WOODS, in chips, small blocks, or chopped, can be used in modern portable pit grills. In 1960 I wasn't that familiar with portable backyard pit grills. Beyond hickory, my knowledge of the various woods to use, starting with oak, began to expand when I dug out and constructed a 2 by 4 foot "Texas pit" in our backyard in Oakland, California. Fresh from the U.S. Air Force, I launched a personal sort of quest that continued into my college years. That is, I longed for, in fact craved, some righteous hickory-*wood*-smoked barbeque just like my Uncle Tom's back in Liberty, Texas. I wound up using oak for the fire in the Texas pit. I found the wood in my father's scrap pile at his furniture repair and cabinet shop. Originally I was looking for hickory wood, but my father said there wasn't any and suggested I use oak pieces instead. I reminded my father that Uncle Tom always used hickory wood. My father insisted that oak wood would work fine.

I remembered Uncle Tom's basic baste and sauce recipes. The ribs and chicken I barbequed with the oak tasted like they had been smoked with *wood* but not hickory. There was also something missing in my baste and sauce. For over two years I tested various ingredients. I was close but I didn't get that delectable flavor of Uncle Tom's hickory-smoked barbeque. It was as if I couldn't get along without a large closed brick pit and several cords of hickory wood like my Uncle Tom (he had died a few years earlier). My hickory quest was now very important to me.

I wound up using a portable pit grill and mixing my pit fire of oak wood with charcoal briquets in an attempt to save the limited amount of oak. One day I discovered *pure* hickory liquid smoke. Fantastic! Opening the bottle and smelling it was almost unbelievable. The hickory smell jumped into my nose with an aromatic power that just wouldn't quit. I bought a large quantity. With anticipation I fired up the pit and poured various amounts of the hickory liquid smoke into my baste-marinade and sauce, using too much at first and testing lesser amounts later.

One day to my surprise I found some hickory wood scrap pieces. I knew I had the right stuff now. I mixed chopped pieces of hickory wood with the charcoal briquets in a newly dug out Texas pit. I even built a cover for the Texas pit. The barbeque was good but not yet Uncle Tom's taste. Through a long process I perfected the baste-marinade, finding the right amounts of lemon juice, vinegar, and hickory liquid smoke and then deciding to add Worcestershire sauce and a small amount of apple juice. (I used the apple juice because I had some notion about fruit wood — which was not available — and I had heard that mesquite wood was sugary and good for barbequing.) During all this information gathering, improvisation, and testing I periodically remembered how my Uncle Tom's brick pit would produce smoke when his baste spilled down on the hickory wood pit fire. Using the portable pit grill I decided one day to soak some hickory wood pieces in my baste-marinade. I spread the precious baste-soaked wood on my white-ash-hot charcoal briquets several times during the barbequing (smoke-pit-cooking) process. When the meat was done I served my family first, savoring the aroma, wanting their reaction.

As my mother and father ate that particular batch of barbeque they commented matter-of-factly, "This bobbyque taste just like Tom Turner's back yonder in Liberty, Texas." Right on time was my thought as I ate. The rest is history and this book – a history of a personal quest – the creatively tested perfection of a contemporary but traditional down-home hickory-smoked "bobbyque" method, using modern portable pit grills.

THE HICKORY CHARCOAL PIT FIRE

The safe and easy way to start a portable pit fire is to presoak your recipe amount of charcoal briquets in a commercial charcoal lighter fluid. **(Do not use gasoline or other volatile substances. They are dangerous and may explode.)** To keep from spraying charcoal lighter fluid on half-lit coals, place the recipe amount of briquets in a large can or glass jar or use a metal bucket. Drop a handful of hickory wood chips in the container. Thoroughly soak the briquets and wood chips with charcoal lighter fluid. *Do not light.* Pile the unlit fluid-soaked briquets and wood chips in a pyramid in the center of the lower charcoal grate of the portable pit grill. Drop a few lit matches on the mound of coals or light with a long twisted piece of paper bag to start the pit fire from a distance. Let the coals burn in the mound, undisturbed, for 10 to 20 minutes until, *one,* the kerosine lighter fluid smell has burned off and, *two,* all the charcoal briquets have turned to a *white-ash-hot.* **(Do not spray or pour lighter fluid on already hot coals.)**

Using long-handle tongs, spread the white-ash-hot coals in a single layer (with some coals on top if necessary) making sure each and every hot coal touches one another for a close bed of coals. With fifty or more white-ash-hot briquets, a pit-thermometer temperature will register 500 degrees Fahrenheit or higher. With your meat entrees ready and waiting, sprinkle evenly the recipe amount of *baste-soaked* or water-soaked hickory wood chips onto the *close* bed of hot coals. Let the soaked wood chips burn into the pit fire until the flames are out, or very lightly spray any persistent flames with water or baste, being careful not to put out the pit fire.

To get the 500-degree temperature down a hundred degrees or so and to extinguish any remaining flames, the best method is to place the pit cover on the grill for a few minutes, leaving the damper vents half open. In a moment or two you should have a flameless hickory briquet fire ready for smoking your entrees. From there add more briquets and soaked hickory wood chips as needed and follow the pit-basting method of the particular recipe you are preparing.

BARBEQUE PIT GRILLS, BRAZIERS, EQUIPMENT, AND SUPPLIES

PIT GRILLS

The best choice among the wide variety of portable pit charcoal grills available is the oval-top kettle model. You can always get a southern hickory-smoke-flavor barbeque entree using a kettle-top pit grill and my recipes and methods. A covered pit grill with damper vents for heat control and a tight-fitting lid encloses the meat you plan to *que.* Since the mid-1970s the kettle-style pit grill has become the most popular. Many of the new kettle models also come with built-in pit thermometers to allow for better heat control.

Many commercialized styles are round, rectangular or square covers but these do not allow for adequate convective smoke-heat circulation like the kettle *oval*-cover pit grill. With the *oval* cover, you can also smoke a 10- to 18-pound turkey.

There are lightweight open braziers such as hibachis, too. Even with these coverless grills you can still get my basic southern-style hickory flavor in your meat entrees. You can always form an aluminum-foil tent and adapt it to an open brazier or hibachi. As long as you marinate your meats, presoak hickory wood chips and spread them over hot charcoal briquets, you can get that delectable hickory-smoked down-home taste.

The wheeled kettle and wagon grills feature air dampers in the bottom and in the lid. You can control ventilation and cooking temperature with these grills. With the lid down, they function like ovens and you can give meat entrees a real smoked quality.

Electric and gas pit grills have covers, but they are quite expensive. They work by the radiant heat principle with volcanic pumice (lava) or ceramic briquets between the gas or electric heat source and the pit grill. They are easy to start and have efficient heat controls. With slightly stronger baste-marinades and more spray basting, you can get a good hickory-smoked flavor in the meat with these types of pits. But the best *contemporary* hickory-smoked barbeque entrees come from the charcoal briquet and hickory wood chip pit-fire method.

BASIC BARBEQUE EQUIPMENT

Tongs: A couple of 18-inch tongs with wooden handles, one for your meat entrees and food and one for hot coals.

Fork: An 18-inch with wooden handle fork. Note that some meats should *not* be forked. Use your second pair of tongs so you don't lose juices. Fully cooked ribs can be forked.

Spatula: An 18-inch spatula with wooden handle. Use it to turn food.

Hinged wire grill basket *(an accessory on some pit grill models):* Use for small steaks, chops, burgers, link sausages, and even hot dogs that require frequent basting and turning.

Basting brush: One with at least a 12-inch, or better an 18-inch handle, for brushbasting entrees and brushing on sauces.

Pot holders: Use for turning a grill basket and adjusting or removing a grill grate from the pit. Also for adjusting pit dampers, removing ash sifters, moving a hot pit, and lifting hot containers.

Spray-Basting Bottles *(comes in 1 and 2 quart sizes):* One or two plastic spray bottles (the kind used to spray plants) with a squeeze trigger and adjustable nozzle. Used to spray-baste entrees with baste-marinade and lightly extinguish any pit flames.

PIT SUPPLIES

Charcoal Briquets: They come in three types, varying from short- to long-burning. Regular coal briquets are not the same as hardwood processed briquets which are made by burning down hardwoods with controlled heat until completely charred and then machine pressing them into briquets. Some wood-processed briquets are manufactured specifically of hickory wood. Regular coal briquets lack the "woodsmoke" factor. Some coal briquets come with an "uncharred" wood core pressed in the center.

Charcoal Lighter Fluid and Solid Starters: Both work well. Most barbeque experts prefer to presoak their charcoal briquets with a commercial kerosine liquid starter. Solid starters provide good starts but sometimes there are flare-ups.

Hickory Wood Chips or Chunks Oak and fruit woods are not as widely sold as mesquite. Hickory is more extensively available than other woods and is sold in bags of hickory wood pieces, chunks, or chips. Hickory wood chunks generally come in 10-pound bags and are becoming more available throughout the country. Hickory chips and pieces usually come in 2-pound bags. Hickory wood can be found in many supermarkets, gardening stores, and super drug stores, especially in the western United States. Some hardware stores also carry them. The combination of hickory wood and hardwood processed charcoal briquets will get you the best contemporary portable pit fire for that traditional outdoor woodsmoked barbeque taste.

BARBEQUING WITH BASTE-MARINADES
(No Cue-B-Rab Allowed)

BARBEQUE SAUCE IS *NOT* BARBEQUE BASTE. Barbeque baste is a better all-around meat marinade. Most storebought barbeque sauces and personal "secret recipe" sauces have a sugar content and should not be used to barbeque meat until it is nearly done. The sugar, honey, or molasses in sauces readily burns under a hot broiler or over a pit of hot coals. Meat burned on the outside, half cooked inside, is often the result, particularly with poultry and pork.

The traditional correct southern-style method for barbequing meats and poultry is with baste-marinades. Some current and old-style barbe*cue* baste recipes, many times used for marinades, are rather bland quick concoctions. Millions who crave some kind of pit-smoked barbeque try their best with a mixture of water, vinegar, and lemon juice, a very basic pit-smoking baste. Others improvise by adding garlic, onions, salt, and pepper...maybe a little Teriyaki or Worcestershire sauce and that's it. But even the most elaborately well-blended barbeque baste recipes of the barbe*cuing* public usually lack a couple of essential contemporary ingredients — *pure* hickory liquid smoke and apple juice. Most baste recipes if liberally used keep the pitqued meats moist and juicy. But juicy, with only a charred flavor, is a long way from that down-home traditional hickory-smoked delicate taste.

"Pit-smoking" and "pit-quing" are words that I use interchangeably throughout this book. "Baste-marinade" is another frequently appearing term. I hope the various hickory-smoke blended baste-marinade recipes included in this book will take you away from that "bottle-back" recipe method using sugar-content sauces on raw or partially cooked meat. The crust of burnt sauce you end up with then is nothing less than what I call "*Cue*-B-Rab." *CUE*-B-RAB? Yes! The process of barbe*cuing* backwards.

 # Uncle Tom's "Bobby-Que" Baste-Marinade

Vegetables
3 cups chopped onions
2 cups chopped red or green bell pepper
1 cup chopped scallions (green onions)
3 cups chopped celery
1 cup chopped hot peppers (optional)
2 cloves garlic minced
Rinds of 5 to 6 lemon cut up (hold seeded lemon juice for
    liquid ingredients)

Staples
1 teaspoon ground black pepper
2 teaspoons seasoning salt
2 teaspoons onion parsley salt
1 teaspoon garlic parsley salt
3 bay leaves

Liquids
1 cup (8 ounces) pure hickory liquid smoke (use 1½ cups
    for stronger hickory flavor)
1½ cups red wine vinegar or cider vinegar
1 cup Worcestershire sauce
2 cups apple juice
1 cup lemon juice (5 to 6 medium-size lemons) or 1 cup
    lime juice
4 quarts water

Place water in an 8-quart pot on high heat. Add all vegetable and staple ingredients, and bring to a boil. Reduce heat to medium and stew for 45 minutes, covered. Remove from heat and let cool. Strain off all stewed ingredients from liquid, and stir in all liquid ingredients. Bring to a boil. Reduce heat to medium low and simmer for 7 minutes, covered. Remove from heat. Room-temperature cool is fine for marinating meat for a few hours, and a 200-degree hot marinade is excellent for a quick hour's marinating.

Yields 4 quarts plus

NOTES: For a stronger, more pungent baste-marinade, use only 3 quarts of water. For stronger still, use only 2 quarts.

• You can prepare baste-marinade as much as a week in advance. Put it in a covered nonmetal container and store in refrigerator.

• This 4-quart plus recipe of my Uncle Tom's all-purpose baste-marinade is enough for a barbeque cookout of ribs for 10 to 15 people. Uncle Tom's Baste-Marinade can also be used to marinate and pit-baste barbequed pork shoulders, butts, pork steaks, chops, poultry, and lamb.

• Add 1 to 1½ cups of strained unused Uncle Tom's Baste-Marinade to any 18- or 28-ounce bottle of store-bought barbeque sauce, stir thoroughly, and simmer for 10 minutes, covered, on medium-low heat. Your storebought barbeque sauce is transformed on contact!

• If pit basting with a spray bottle, open bottom inside end of suction tube with a sharp knife so baste flows easily to liberally baste meat.

 # Worcestershire Wine Herbal Baste-Marinade

Vegetables
3 cups chopped onions
2 cups chopped red or green bell pepper
1 cup chopped scallions (green onions)
2 cups chopped celery
3 cloves garlic minced

Staples
1 teaspoon each ground black pepper, seasoning salt,
    garlic parsley salt
2 bay leaves
1 tablespoon oregano leaves
1 tablespoon crumbled dry rosemary
3 cubes or 2 teaspoons beef bouillon extract

Liquids
1 cup dry red cooking wine
½ cup red wine vinegar
½ cup onion wine (optional if not available)
1 cup Worcestershire sauce
½ cup (4 ounces) of pure hickory liquid smoke
½ cup fresh lemon juice, seeded
3 quarts water

Combine vegetable and staple ingredients in water in a 6-quart pot on high heat. Bring to a boil. Reduce heat to medium and stew for 40 minutes, covered. Set aside and let cool. Strain off all stewed ingredients, including bay leaves, from liquid in pot and stir in all liquid ingredients. Bring to a quick boil and immediately turn off heat. Store in refrigerator if not ready to use.

Yields 3 Quarts plus

NOTES: For a stronger beef baste-marinade use only 2 quarts of water.

This recipe can serve a barbeque cookout for 15 pounds of beef roast or 3 to 5 slabs (9 to 15 pounds) of beef spareribs. Use exactly half of all vegetable, staple, and liquid ingredients for pit-que'n smaller single 3- to 6-pound roasts or 1 to 2 slabs of beef ribs.

Hickory Herbal Tomato-Onion Baste-Marinade

This particular baste-marinade recipe is next door to a sauce except it has no sugar content. Refrigerated overnight marinating to excellent, it affords any beef, pork, or poultry entree a *saucy* pit basting for total "que'n" times.

Vegetables
2 cups chopped Spanish onions
2 cups chopped scallions (green onions)
1 cup chopped red or green bell pepper
2 cups chopped celery
2 cloves garlic minced
Rinds of 3 limes, cut up (hold juice for liquid ingredients)

Staples
1 tablespoon onion powder
1 teaspoon ground black pepper
1 tablespoon celery salt
1 teaspoon hickory smoke salt (if unavailable, substitute
    seasoning salt)
1 teaspoon dry mustard
3 bay leaves
2 tablespoons blended Italian herbs

Liquids
2 cups canned tomato juice or V-8 juice
1/2 cup Worcestershire sauce

¾ cup dry red sherry wine
¼ cup onion wine (optional if not available)
¾ cup red wine vinegar
Juice of 3 limes, seeded
1 cup (8 ounces) pure hickory liquid smoke
2 quarts water

Combine vegetable and staple ingredients in water in a 6-quart pot on high heat. Bring to a boil. Reduce heat to medium and stew for 40 minutes, covered. Set aside and let cool. Strain off stewed ingredients from liquid and stir in all liquid ingredients. Bring to a quick boil, reduce heat to medium low, and simmer for 12 minutes, stirring periodically. Remove from heat.
Yields 2½ quarts plus

Lime-Mint Garlic-Onion Baste-Marinade

Pit-smoked lamb or pork entrees with this baste-marinade are "onionized" with a blended garlic and hickory lime-mint accent.

Vegetables
3 cups chopped onions
1 cup chopped scallions
1 cup chopped red or green bell pepper
2 cups chopped celery
4 cloves garlic minced
½ cup chopped onion-garlic (optional if not available)
7 or 8 fresh mint leaves (use whole)
7 whole lime rinds, cut up (hold juice for liquid
    ingredients)

Staples
2 tablespoons onion parsley salt
1 tablespoon seasoning salt
1 tablespoon ground black pepper

Liquids
1 cup red wine vinegar
½ cup (4 ounces) pure hickory liquid smoke
½ cup onion wine (optional if not available)
1 cup fresh lime juice, seeded (approximately 7 limes)
2 quarts water

Place water in a 6-quart pot on high heat. Add all vegetable and staple ingredients, and bring to a boil. Reduce heat to medium and stew for 35 minutes, covered. Remove from heat. Stir in all liquid ingredients. Bring to a boil and immediately turn heat to medium low. Let the baste-marinade simmer for 5 minutes only, covered.

Yields 2¹/₂ quarts

NOTE: For small cookouts of lamb or pork entrees, exactly half of all ingredients yields 1¹/₄ quarts.

 # Lemon-Orange-Pineapple Baste-Marinade

This recipe is a mouth-watering treat for 12 to 20 servings (8 to 12 pounds) of pit-smoked pork roast, country-style ribs, or ham steaks.

Vegetables
    3 cups chopped scallions (green onions)
    1 cup chopped red or green bell pepper
    2 cups chopped celery

Staples
    1 teaspoon garlic parsley salt
    1 teaspoon onion parsley salt
    1 teaspoon ground black pepper
    ¹/₂ teaspoon ground cloves (double amount if desired)

Liquids
    2 cups pineapple juice
    1 cup fresh lemon juice, seeded
    2 cups fresh orange juice, seeded
    1 cup cider vinegar
    ³/₄ cup (6 ounces) pure hickory liquid smoke
    2 quarts of water

Combine vegetable and staple ingredients in water in a 6-quart pot on high heat. Bring to a boil. Reduce to medium heat and stew for 35 minutes, covered. Remove from heat and strain off stewed vegetables. Stir all liquid ingredients and simmer for 7 minutes, covered. Remove from heat and let cool, or refrigerate if not ready to use.

Yields 3 quarts

Spicy Hot Hickory-Pepper Baste-Marinade

With this baste-marinade recipe you can actually season the meat or poultry entree down to the bone with a *hot* spicy taste beforehand, then brush on barbeque *sauce* during the last 20 minutes of que'n time.

Vegetables
  2 cups chopped Texas or Spanish onion
  1 cup chopped hot jalapeño peppers
  1 cup chopped red bell peppers
  2 cups chopped celery
  1 cup chopped hot peppers
  1/2 cup chopped onion-garlic (if not available use 2 cloves garlic, minced)

Staples
  1 tablespoon pure ground hot red chili pepper
  2 tablespoons chili powder (hot taste)
  1 teaspoon ground cumin
  1 teaspoon ground Mexican oregano (use regular if Mexican not available)
  1 tablespoon spicy dry mustard (or substitute hot spicy mustard)
  4 cubes or 3 teaspoons beef bouillon extract (substitute chicken bouillon extract for poultry)

Liquids
  1 1/4 cup (10 ounces) pure hickory liquid smoke
  2 tablespoons hot pepper sauce (optional)
  1/2 cup hot pepper juice
  1/2 cup Worcestershire sauce
  1 cup red wine vinegar
  1 cup fresh lemon juice, seeded
  3 quarts water

Combine vegetable and staple ingredients in water in a 6-quart pot on high heat. Bring to a boil. Reduce heat to medium high and stew for 30 minutes, covered. Set aside and let cool. Strain off stewed vegetables and stir in all liquid ingredients. Bring to a quick boil, reduce heat, and simmer on a medium-low heat for 7 minutes only.

Yields 3 quarts plus

Hickory-Quick Barbeque Baste-Marinade

When you don't have a lot of leisure time but have a craving, try the following barbeque baste recipe for pit-baste smoking. It gives a hickory-smoke flavor to almost any meat or poultry entree you desire.

> 1 cup cider vinegar or red wine vinegar
> 1/2 cup fresh lemon juice, seeded (use rinds cut up in pot)
> 3/4 to 1 cup (6 to 8 ounces) pure hickory liquid smoke
> 1 cup red cooking wine (optional)
> 1 tablespoon *each* liquid garlic and liquid onion (or chop
>   2 onions)
> 1 cup Worcestershire sauce or 1/2 cup of Teriyaki sauce
> 1 cup apple juice or cranberry juice
> 1 quart of water

Combine all ingredients with water in a 4-quart pot on medium-high heat. Stir and bring to a boil, cover and boil 5 minutes. Remove from heat and strain off lemon rinds or any cooked onions. Refrigerate if not ready to use immediately as hot marinade.

Strain and use in spray bottle for basting pit-smoked meats, especially pit grilled pork ribs, beef ribs, pork chops, pork and beef steaks, lamb chops, poultry, grilled burgers, and pork and beef roasts. The spray-basting also helps control flames in the pit-fire when not overused. For a real hickory-smoke flavor, pre-soak any amount of hickory wood chips in a cup or so of this basic marinade.

Yields 1 1/2 quarts

NOTE: Marinate meat in 200-degree hot marinade for 20 minutes for super-quick and tasty results.

WHAT'S IN MY BARBEQUE SAUCES?

THE BARBEQUE SAUCE RECIPES THAT FOLLOW are enough to serve ten to twelve people. In some cases, you will have sauce remaining for another barbeque. The sauces can be prepared one to two days ahead and stored in the refrigerator for five to six days, or frozen in a plastic container for up to two months. Sauce refrigerated for one or two days is zestier. Just as storing chili enhances its flavor the same thing happens when barbeque sauce is refrigerated. The blended spices, various vegetable ingredients, vinegars, herbs, wines, and pure hickory liquid smoke are all accentuated in the pit-qued entrees when sauces sit a couple of days before using.

Do not use aluminum foil as a cover *touching* the sauce when storing it for a long period. The sauce recipes have an acid base (lemon, vinegar, tomato) that will eat holes in the foil. This also will taint the flavor of the sauce and of saucy meats wrapped in foil.

Although my Hickory-Herbal Barbeque Sauce recipe is salt-free and sugarless, most of the recipes do contain various salt ingredients. When preparing the sauces, you can add your salt or salts after the sauce has finished brewing. The sauces are stirred and cooked down for a quasi-thick consistency. The concentration of flavors can also cause the sauces to become slightly saltier.

The barbeque methods described in this guide largely call for the application of sauce when the meats are practically done. Sugar sweeteners in "secret" sauces and in store-bought barbeque sauces will burn over hot pit fires. My sauces (except for the sugarless herbal sauce) contain various sweeteners of brown sugar, honey or molasses and will also burn if put on meat entrees too soon.

Barbeque'n with Bobby is an attempt to demonstrate my contemporary traditional "que'n" method and to halt the shake-and-bake, "bottleback" recipe methods of preparing so-called *barbeque*. The general barbeque information floating around reflects an oniony and garlicky misunderstanding of how to prepare ribs, poultry, links, burgers, and steaks. This commercialized misunderstanding has also insulted our taste buds. For righteously good southern, Texas style hickory-smoke barbeque, we cannot continue with the bottleback recipe method of putting storebought barbeque sauce on raw meat and slapping it under the oven broiler or over a hot pit of charcoal. Unless you are a pit master who has perfected such a method of barbequing, you should avoid this approach.

In this hickory-smoke pit-basting barbeque guide, I place barbeque sauces in the same category as gravies when it comes to "que'n" meats on the pit. The real traditionally savored flavor of down-home hickory-smoke barbeque is *in the meat* (after the marinating pit-basting process) *not* in the sauce. Zesty spicy-tasty sauces are added to seasoned entrees. While millions of people love meat entrees spiced with savory sauces, sauces should actually be brushed on the meats during the last minutes of pit cooking and served hot with the barbeque meal.

 ## Bobby's Spicy Barbeque Sauce

This sauce can be made either very hot or just a little hot. Use all or any of the hot ingredients and in any amount you want.

Vegetables
    1 cup onions, (preferably Spanish), finely chopped
    ½ cup scallions (green onions), finely chopped
    ¾ cup red or green bell pepper, finely chopped
    1 cup celery finely chopped
    ½ cup carrot finely grated
    2 cloves garlic, minced
    (Ingredients *finely* cut up or *pureed in blender* and rinsed
        from blender with 1 cup of water)

Staples
    1 teaspoon *each* garlic parsley salt, seasoning salt, black
        pepper, blended Italian herb seasoning, and cayenne
        pepper
    3 tablespoons dry spicy mustard (or substitute ⅓ cup
        prepared brown mustard)

1 cup packed dark brown sugar melted in ½ cup hot tap water (or use 1 cup honey or 1 cup molasses and no water)

2 tablespoons pure ground mild red chili powder

Liquids

1 quart V-8 juice (or use 28 to 30 ounce can stewed tomatoes, or use 4 to 5 fresh tomatoes chopped and pureed)

2 6-ounce cans (1½ cups) tomato paste

¾ cup red wine vinegar (or to taste)

¾ cup fresh lemon juice, seeded

¾ cup dry red (cooking) wine

½ cup spicy brown prepared mustard

½ cup Worcestershire Sauce (or to taste)

1 cup of pure hickory liquid smoke (or more to taste)

½ cup melted margarine

2 cups water (note: one cup from rinsed blender above)

HOT TASTE OPTIONS:

3 hot jalapeño peppers, chopped (or added to blender and pureed with vegetables)

2 tablespoons crushed dried peppers or ⅓ cup Tabasco Sauce

½ cup spicy prepared brown mustard

For mildly hot taste, add only half of very hot ingredients or season to hot taste desired.

Combine vegetable ingredients and first cup water (from rinsed blender) and melted margarine in a 6-quart pot on medium-high heat. Saute for 3 minutes uncovered. Add V-8 juice or pureed tomatoes, stirring thoroughly. Add second cup of water and all remaining staple and liquid ingredients, stirring thoroughly. Add hot taste ingredients (seasoned to taste). Bring to a boil and reduce heat to medium-low. Simmer uncovered for 1 hour stirring frequently or until sauce begins to thicken. Remove from heat and refrigerate or freeze in plastic container until ready to use. (Use 1 cup of baste-marinade or water when warming up frozen stored sauces).

Yields Approx. 1¾ quarts

Hickory-Quick Barbeque Sauce

Use the hot-taste options in the amounts suggested or in any combination or amount you desire.

> 1$\frac{1}{2}$ cup (12 ounces) tomato paste
> 1 quart V-8 juice (or tomato juice or puree 3 or 4 chopped
>   fresh tomatoes)
> $\frac{3}{4}$ cup (up to 6 ounces) pure hickory liquid smoke
> $\frac{3}{4}$ cup red wine vinegar
> 1 cup apple juice
> $\frac{3}{4}$ cup fresh lemon juice, seeded
> $\frac{3}{4}$ cup pure carrot juice
> 1 cup Worcestershire sauce
> 2 tablespoons liquid onion
> 5 tablespoons prepared mustard
> 2 tablespoons liquid garlic
> $\frac{3}{4}$ cup packed brown sugar melted in $\frac{1}{2}$ cup hot tap water
>   (or use $\frac{3}{4}$ cup honey or molasses and no water)
> 2 teaspoons ground black pepper
> 2 teaspoons Italian herb seasoning
> 2 teaspoons seasoning salt

HOT TASTE OPTIONS
> 2 tablespoons spicy hot brown prepared mustard
> $\frac{1}{2}$ cup dry crushed red pepper
> $\frac{1}{4}$ cup Tabasco or regular hot sauce (or to taste)

Pour V-8 or tomato juice (or pureed tomatoes) into a 5-quart pot and add all other ingredients on high heat. Stir thoroughly and continuously, bringing to a boil. Reduce heat to medium low. Stirring periodically , simmer for 35 minutes or until sauce begins to thicken. Set sauce aside until ready to use.

Yields 1$\frac{1}{2}$ quarts
NOTE: For $\frac{3}{4}$ quart use exactly $\frac{1}{2}$ of each ingredient.

Apple-Lime-Mint Barbeque Sauce

For lamb, Cornish hens, and various pork entrees this low sodium recipe of fresh vegetables and fruit barbequing is a winner when brushed on entrees during the last 20 minutes of barbequing time.

  1 pound (3 medium) tomatoes, finely chopped or pureed
  1 cup green onions, finely chopped or pureed
  2 medium green cooking apples, cored, peeled, and finely
      chopped or pureed
  8 fresh mint leaves, minced or pureed
  1 tablespoon *each* blended herb seasoning, lemon pepper
      seasoning
  ½ cup *each* celery, bell pepper, carrot, (finely chopped or
      pureed)
  ½ cup (4 ounces) hickory liquid smoke (or slightly more
      to taste)
  ½ cup honey
  3 tablespoons spicy hot prepared mustard
  ½ cup Worcestershire sauce
  ½ cup red wine vinegar
  ¾ cup fresh lime juice, seeded
  2 cups "mint tea" water (use 3 or 4 mint tea bags)

HOT TASTE OPTION
  ½ cup jalapeño peppers, finely chopped or pureed

In a 6-quart pot combine mint tea water, finely chopped or pureed tomatoes, green onions, apples, celery, mint leaves, seasonings, bell pepper, carrot and Jalapeño pepper if used, on high heat. Bring to a boil, stirring thoroughly.

With heat still on high, add remaining ingredients, again stirring thoroughly. Reduce heat to medium and cover. Stir every 5 minutes and cook for 45 minutes or until sauce thickens. Remove from heat and let cool or refrigerate overnight.

Yields 2 quarts plus

DECLARATION: BARBEQUE BILL OF RIGHTS

WHEN IN THE COURSE OF HUMAN DEVELOPMENT it becomes necessary for us, the citizens of the earth, to creatively improve the culinary art of barbe-que'n in our opposition to the overly commercialized bondage of "cue-be-rab" (barbecuing backwards); and to assume, within the realm of palatable biological reactions to which the laws of nature and nature's God entitle us, a decent respect for all the billions of human taste buds and savory barbeque desires; we the people declare a basic barbeque bill of rights which impels us to help halt, eradicate, and ultimately stamp out "cue-be-rab!"

As the commercialized backwards "bottle-back" recipe methods pursue and invariably evince a design to reduce our backyard-picnics into burnt, half done, bland, badly seasoned, improperly pit-qued entrees, then it is the right of we the barbeque lovers of the world, to alter the cue-be-rab phenomenon and creatively change our recipe process for a more righteous saucy, down-home, wood-smoking, delectable, baste-marinating, barbeque'n methodology.

THE BASIC "RIGHTS" OF HICKORY SMOKE PIT BOBBY-QUE'N

CERTAIN "RIGHTS" ARE ABSOLUTELY BASIC to pit-smoking. You'll see them repeatedly in the recipes that follow, but here they are in summary form. If you follow these basic steps, your barbequed meats will always come out tasting *qued* down to the bone.

1. Preparing Baste-Marinades: Always use recipe amounts of hickory liquid smoke.

2. Marinating Meat Entrees: 30-minute hot marinade, or 4 hours at room temperature or overnight in refrigerator.

3. Baste-Soaking Hickory Wood Chips: Spread out over *white-ash-hot* charcoals for smoke-flavor barbequing.

4. Sear Seasoning: Browning and sealing in any coated meat seasonings before pit-basting.

5. Constant Basting: Baste meat entrees with blended hickory flavored marinade (do not use sugar content sauces).

6. Cover Top Pit: Keep down after each basting method and adding more baste-soaked hickory wood chips as needed.

7. Glaze on Barbeque Sauces: Only after meat entree is mostly cooked and/or done.

HICKORY-SMOKED BARBEQUE BEEF

Hickory-Qued Beef Rib Roast

4- to 6-pound beef rib roast
3/4 teaspoon (approximately) *each* onion parsley salt,
   seasoning salt, paprika (from shakers)
1 1/2 quarts Onion Wine Baste-Marinade (recipe follows)
1/2 pound of hickory wood chips, baste-soaked

TO PREPARE ONION WINE BASTE-MARINADE

Vegetables
1 cup *each* Spanish onions, green onions, bell peppers,
   celery, chopped
1 clove garlic, minced

Staples
1 teaspoon *each* onion powder, black pepper, onion
   parsley salt, celery salt

Liquids
1 cup dry red wine
1/3 cup onion wine (substitute onion juice)
3/4 cup red wine vinegar
3/4 cup (6 ounces) pure hickory liquid smoke
1/2 cup carrot juice
1/2 cup Worcestershire sauce
1 1/2 quarts water

Combine vegetable and staple ingredients and water in a 6-quart pot on high heat. Bring to a boil. Reduce heat to medium. Stew for 35 minutes, covered. Remove from heat and let cool. Strain off stewed ingredients from liquid and stir in ingredients. Bring to a quick boil. Reduce heat to medium low and simmer for 7 minutes. Cool.

Yields 1¹/₂ quarts plus

TO MARINATE RIB ROAST

Place roast in a deep close-fitting pot or bowl or in a sturdy plastic bag set in rimmed pan. Pour approximately half of baste-marinade over roast, covering it. Cover container or twist-tie plastic bag. Marinate for 2 to 3 hours at room temperature or refrigerate overnight. Turn occasionally for thorough marinating.

PIT FIRE

Presoak hickory wood chips for 30 minutes in 1 cup of baste-marinade and drain. Spread half of soaked chips over a close bed of 40-odd white-ash-hot charcoal briquets. Let burn into fire until flames are out.

Adjust dampers half to fully open. After sear seasoning, evenly bank coals around an 8-inch drip pan. (Midway through cooking time, add 10 to 12 briquets and spread remaining soaked hickory chips over *white-ash-hot* charcoal briquets.)

SEAR SEASONING

When pit fire is ready, remove roast from marinade and drain. (Retain used marinade for pit-basting.) From shakers, sprinkle light coats of onion parsley salt, seasoning salt, and paprika over all sides of roast. With fingers and hands, press in coated seasonings. Grease pit grill lightly. Place roast on pit grill 4 to 6 inches above hot pit fire. Brown 3 to 5 minutes on each side, searing and sealing in coated seasonings.

PIT BASTING

Spray- or brush-baste roast, turning and basting again every 15 minutes for 1 hour for rare meat. Dampers should be half to fully open and pit top closed after each basting.

For medium rare, cook an extra 30 minutes or until done the way you like it, liberally basting. Serve with sauce if desired.

Makes 6 to 8 servings

Saucy Beef Spareribs

10 to 12 pounds beef spareribs, cut in 2- or 3-rib pieces
2½ quarts Hickory Herbal Tomato Onion Baste-Marinade
    (page 16)
1 quart of barbeque sauce desired (pages 22 to 25)
½ pound hickory wood chips, watersoaked

TO MARINATE BEEF RIBS
Place cut rib pieces in a close-fitting container or in a sturdy plastic bag set in a rimmed pan. Pour in enough baste-marinade to submerge ribs (approximately 1 quart). Cover container or twist-tie plastic bag. Marinate for 2 hours at room temperature or refrigerate overnight. Turn occasionally for thorough marinating.

PIT FIRE
Presoak hickory wood chips in 2 cups of water for 30 minutes and drain. Spread half of soaked chips over a close bed of 50-odd white-ash-hot charcoal briquets. Allow soaked chips to burn into pit fire until flames are out. Add several charcoal briquets as needed and spread second half of soaked wood chips on pit fire midway through cooking time.

PIT BASTING
Spray- or brush-baste ribs, turning and basting every 20 minutes for 1½ to 2 hours or until done the way you like them. Adjust dampers fully open, closing pit cover after each basting. During last 20 minutes of cooking time, brush on desired barbeque sauce every 5 minutes. Serve immediately with remaining sauce.
Makes 10 to 12 servings

Worcestershire-Sherry Chuck Roast

5- to 6-pound chuck roast, cut 2½ to 3 inches thick
1½ quarts Worcestershire-Sherry Herbal Baste-Marinade
    (recipe follows)
½ pound hickory wood chips, baste-soaked

TO PREPARE WORCESTERSHIRE-SHERRY
HERBAL BASTE-MARINADE

Vegetables

   1 cup *each* onions, scallions, celery, bell peppers,
      chopped
   2 cloves garlic, minced

Staples

   1 teaspoon *each* dry rosemary, dry mustard, basil,
      oregano leaves, black pepper, seasoning salt, garlic
      parsley salt
   2 bay leaves

Liquids

   ¾ cups (6 ounces) pure hickory liquid smoke
   1 cup dry sherry
   1 cup Worcestershire sauce
   ¼ cup red wine vinegar
   ½ cup fresh lemon juice, seeded
   ¼ cup salad oil
   1 quart water

Combine vegetable and staple ingredients in water in a 6-quart pot on high heat. Bring to a boil. Reduce heat to medium. Stew for 35 minutes, covered. Set aside and let cool. Strain off stewed ingredients from liquid and stir in all liquid ingredients. Simmer for 7 minutes on low heat.

   Yields 1½ quarts plus

TO MARINATE CHUCK ROAST

Place roast in a sizable close-fitting container or use a sturdy plastic bag set in a rimmed container. Pour approximately half of baste-marinade over roast. Cover container or twist-tie plastic bag. Marinate for 2 hours at room temperature or refrigerate overnight. Turn occasionally for thorough marinating.

PIT FIRE

Presoak hickory wood chips in 1½ cups of baste-marinade for 30 minutes and drain. Spread half of soaked chips over solid bed of 40-odd white-ash-hot charcoal briquets. Allow chips to burn into fire until flames are out. Add remaining chips midway through cooking time. Adjust damper vents three-fourths closed.

PIT BASTING

When pit fire is ready, remove roast from marinade and drain. (Retain used baste-marinade for pit-basting.) Place roast on lightly greased grill 4 to 6 inches above pit fire. Brown 3 to 5 minutes on each side. Liberally spray- or brush-baste, turning every 10 minutes, for 40 minutes for rare meat, or cook until done the way you like it. Slice across grain and serve with sauce desired.

Makes 6 to 8 servings

Skewered Hickory-Qued Sirloin

4 to 6 pounds sirloin steak, cut in 1- to 2-inch cubes
2 large bell peppers, cut in 1- to 2-inch squares
2 medium onions (quartercut peeled onion, 2 or 3 layers
    per piece)
1/2 pound mushrooms, each sliced in half
2 quarts Worcestershire Wine-Herbal Baste-Marinade
    made with only 2 cups water (page 15)
1/2 pound hickory wood chips, baste-soaked

TO MARINATE SIRLOIN

Place sirloin cubes, halved mushrooms, bell pepper squares, and onion pieces in a bowl or pot or a plastic bag set in a rimmed container. Pour half of baste-marinade over meat and vegetables, submerging. Cover container or twist-tie plastic bag. Marinate for 2 hours at room temperature or refrigerate overnight.

PIT FIRE

Presoak hickory wood chips in 2 cups of baste-marinade for 30 minutes and drain. Spread soaked chips evenly over close bed of 40-odd white-ash-hot charcoal briquets. Let chips burn into pit fire until flames are out.

SKEWERING

Drain baste-marinade from sirloin and vegetables. (Strain and retain used marinade for pit-basting.) Divide meat equally among 8 to 10 sturdy skewers. Place a piece of pepper and a piece of onion between pieces of meat; add a piece of mushroom next to every other piece of meat. (If desired, skewer 3 whole salad tomatoes and/or other vegetable pieces.)

PIT BASTING

Place "kabobed" skewers on lightly greased pit grill, 4 to 6 inches above pit fire. Turning skewers regularly, brown and liberally spray or brush-baste meat every 5 minutes for 20 minutes for rare (pit cover down after basting) or until done the way you like sirloin. Serve immediately with barbeque sauce if desired.

Makes 8 to 10 servings

Spicy Hot Hickory-Qued Short Ribs

6 pounds lean beef short ribs, cracked
2 quarts Hickory Herbal Tomato-Onion Baste-Marinade
  (page 16) with hot-taste ingredients added (recipe
  follows)
1 quart Bobby's Spicy Barbeque Sauce (page 22)
$\frac{1}{2}$ pound hickory wood chips, baste-soaked

Baste-Marinade Made Spicy Hot
$\frac{1}{2}$ cup hot pepper juice
1 tablespoon ground hot red chili pepper
1 tablespoon hot chili powder

Add to baste-marinade and mix thoroughly.

TO MARINATE SHORT RIBS
Place short ribs in a sizable tight-fitting container or in a sturdy plastic bag set in a rimmed pan. Pour in about $\frac{1}{2}$ quart of baste-marinade to cover them. Cover container or twist-tie plastic bag, pulling in close to submerge ribs. Marinate at room temperature for 2 hours or refrigerate overnight. Turn occasionally for thorough marinating.

PIT FIRE
Presoak hickory wood chips in 2 cups of baste for 20 minutes and drain. Spread half of soaked chips evenly over a close bed of 50-odd white-ash-hot charcoal briquets. Let chips burn into pit fire until flames are out. Add rest of soaked chips midway through cooking time. Adjust damper vents $\frac{1}{4}$ open the first half of cooking time and $\frac{3}{4}$ open the last half of cooking time.

PIT BASTING
Remove short ribs from baste-marinade and drain slightly. (Retain used marinade for pit-basting.) Place short ribs on lightly greased pit grill 4 to 6 inches above pit fire and brown 2 to 3 minutes on each side. Spray- or brush-baste liberally, then turn and baste every 20 minutes (pit cover down after each basting) for 60 minutes or until done the way you like barbequed short ribs. Brush on desired hot or mild barbeque sauce or fork-dip in sauce every

5 minutes for last 20 minutes of cooking. Serve immediately with remaining sauce.

Makes 6 to 8 servings

Hickory Pit-Smoked Meat Loaf

3 to 4 pounds lean ground beef or ground sirloin
1/2 pound hickory wood chips, baste-soaked

Meat Seasoning

1/2 teaspoon *each* ground red chili pepper, garlic parsley
    powder, onion powder
1 packet onion soup mix
3/4 cup onions, finely chopped
3/4 cup red or green bell peppers, finely chopped, or
    blender pureed
1 cup celery, finely chopped, or blender pureed
3/4 cup carrot, finely grated carrot, or blender pureed
1 cup (8 ounces) tomato paste
1/3 cup (3 ounces) pure hickory liquid smoke
4 tablespoons Worcestershire sauce or soy sauce
2 large eggs, well beaten

TO PREPARE BASTE

1/3 cup (3 ounces) liquid hickory smoke
1/2 cup Worcestershire sauce
1/2 cup red wine vinegar
1/2 cup fresh lemon juice, seeded and strained
1 cup cooking sherry wine
1 quart water

Combine all baste ingredients and water in a 4-quart pot on high heat. Bring to a boil and remove from heat and let cool.

Yields approximately 2 quarts

PIT FIRE

Mix 1 cup of baste with 1 cup of water and presoak hickory wood chips for 20 minutes. Drain. Spread soaked chips over a close bed of 50-odd white-ash-hot charcoal briquets. Adjust damper vents half closed.

TO MIX AND SHAPE LOAF

In a sizable bowl, thoroughly mix beef with red chili pepper, garlic parsley powder, onion powder, and onion soup mix. Using your hands add and mix thoroughly finely chopped or pureed vegetables, tomato paste, liquid smoke, Worcestershire or soy sauce. Add beaten eggs and mix thoroughly. Place meat loaf on a square or round aluminum throwaway pan. Shape to size and thickness desired.

ON THE PIT

Place pan on pit grill 4 to 6 inches above pit fire. Let cook with pit cover down for 15 to 20 minutes, then liberally brush- or spray-baste every 10 to 15 minutes for 1½ hours or until meat loaf is done. Serve immediately with barbeque sauce if desired.

Makes 6 to 8 servings

Hickory Marinated Steak

4 to 6 each T-bone or porterhouse or sirloin steaks, cut to
    desired thickness
3 cups Butter Hickory Marinade (recipe follows)
1 quart Hickory-Quick Barbeque Sauce (page 24)
1 teaspoon *each* onion parsley powder, ground black
    pepper, celery seed
½ pound hickory wood chips, baste-soaked

TO PREPARE BUTTER HICKORY MARINADE

¾ cube butter or margarine
¾ cup (6 ounces) pure hickory liquid smoke
1 cup dry red wine or cooking sherry
½ cup Worcestershire sauce
½ cup pure carrot juice
½ cup fresh lemon juice or lime juice, seeded
3 cups of water

Set butter or margarine aside. In a 2-quart sauce pan over medium heat, combine all other ingredients in water. Simmer covered for 5 minutes. Remove from heat. Separate out 1 cup of baste to soak hickory wood chips. Stir butter or margarine into remaining hot marinade.

Yields approximately 4 cups

TO MARINATE STEAKS

While marinade is still hot, coat bottom of a tight-fitting container or a 2-inch rimmed rectangular pan and place steaks. Liberally brush baste-marinade all over each steak. Pour remaining marinade over steaks. Marinate at room temperature 1 to 2 hours or refrigerate overnight.

PIT FIRE

Presoak hickory wood chips in separate cup of baste for 30 minutes and drain. Spread soaked chips over close bed of 50-odd white-ash-hot charcoal briquets. Let soaked chips burn into pit fire until flames are out. Adjust damper vents fully open.

PIT BASTING

When pit fire is ready, remove steaks from marinade and drain. (Retain any Butter Hickory Marinade for brush-basting in pit.) Sprinkle light coats of onion-parsley powder, ground black pepper, and celery seed on both sides of steaks. Sear and brown one minute on each side, sealing in coated seasoning. Baste and turn every three minutes for a total of 10 minutes for rare meat (pit cover top down), or cook and baste until done the way you like them.

Makes 4 to 6 servings

Sherry Hickory Tenderloin Roast

4 to 6 pounds filet of beef
1½ quart Hickory-Wine Baste-Marinade (recipe follows)
½ pound hickory wood chips, baste-soaked

TO PREPARE HICKORY WINE BASTE-MARINADE

½ cube butter or margarine
½ cup (4 ounces) pure hickory liquid smoke
¼ cup *each* finely chopped green onions, finely chopped
      parsley, grated carrot, all blender pureed together
1½ cups cooking sherry
⅓ cup fresh lemon or lime juice, seeded
3 tablespoons onion juice or 3 tablespoons onion powder
½ cup Worcestershire sauce
3 cups water

Set butter or margarine aside. In a 3-quart pot, combine all other baste-marinade ingredients with water on high heat. Bring to a quick boil. Remove from heat. Separate out 1 cup of baste-marinade to soak hickory wood chips. Add butter or margarine to remaining baste. Simmer on low medium heat for 7 minutes, covered. Remove from heat and let cool.

TO MARINATE ROAST

In a tight-fitting container or sturdy plastic bag, pour baste-marinade over filet of beef. Marinate for 2 hours at room temperature or refrigerate overnight. One hour before cooking, remove filet roast and slightly drain. (Strain and retain used marinade for pit-basting.) Roll against grain of meat and tie string to hold shape. Wrap roast in foil and refrigerate at 33 degrees for about 30 minutes until firm.

PIT FIRE

Presoak hickory wood chips in reserved baste-marinade for 30 minutes and drain. Spread soaked chips evenly over a close bed of 50-odd white-ash-hot charcoal briquets. Let chips burn into pit fire until flames are out. Adjust damper vents half open.

PIT BASTING

Remove filet roast from foil wrapping. Place roast on lightly greased pit grill 4 to 6 inches above pit fire. Turn and brush- or spray-baste, roast every 7 minutes for 35 minutes for rare. (Close pit cover after each basting.) Or cook until done the way you like it. Cut serving across grain in thickness desired and serve with any sauce or condiment desired.

Makes 5 to 8 servings

Hickory Chili Pit-Qued Blade Roast

4- to 6-pound blade roast, cracked and cut 2 to 2½ inches
    thick
1 teaspoon mild chili powder (from shaker)
1½ quarts Hickory Chili Baste-Marinade (recipe follows)
Hot or Mild Barbeque Sauce (pages 22 to 25)
¼ pound hickory wood chips, baste-soaked

TO PREPARE HICKORY CHILI BASTE-MARINADE

½ cup (4 ounces) pure hickory liquid smoke
½ cup red wine vinegar
¾ cup Worcestershire sauce
½ cup fresh lemon juice, seeded
2 tablespoons liquid garlic (or mince 2 garlic cloves)

1 tablespoon ground oregano (Mexican if available)
1 teaspoon *each* garlic parsley salt, seasoning salt
1 tablespoon *each* onion powder and ground chili powder
    (hot or mild)
3/4 cup tomato-based chili sauce
4 cups water

Set aside chili sauce. Combine all other ingredients in water in a 4-quart pot on high heat. Bring to a boil and reduce heat to medium. Simmer for 5 minutes. Remove from heat and separate out 1 1/2 cups for baste-soaking the hickory wood chips. Add chili sauce to hot remaining marinade and stir. Let cool.

Yields 1 1/2 quarts

TO MARINATE ROAST

Place roast in a tight-fitting pot or container or use a sturdy plastic bag set in a rimmed container. Pour approximately half of baste-marinade over roast, covering it. Cover container or twist-tie plastic bag. Marinate for 4 hours at room temperature or refrigerate overnight.

PIT FIRE

Presoak hickory wood chips in reserved baste for 30 minutes and drain. Spread soaked chips over close bed of 50-odd white-ash-hot charcoal briquets. Let chips burn into fire until flames are out.

SEAR SEASONING

When pit fire is ready, remove roast from marinade and drain. (Retain used marinade for pit-basting.) From shaker, sprinkle light coat of mild chili powder on roast. Place roast 4 to 6 inches above pit fire on lightly greased grill. Sear, brown, and seal in seasonings for 3 to 5 minutes on each side.

PIT BASTING

After searing, liberally brush on baste, turn and baste again. Then baste every 10 to 15 minutes, closing pit cover after each basting, for 50 minutes for rare. Or cook until done the way you like blade roast. Brush on a couple coats of barbeque sauce, each side, during last 10 minutes of cooking time. Serve with remaining sauce.

Makes 6 to 8 servings

Hickory Teriyaki Pit-Qued Flank Steak
(with Mushrooms)

2 flank steaks (about 7 pounds total)
1/2 pound mushrooms, washed and sliced
1 quart Hickory Teriyaki Baste-Marinade (recipe follows)
1 cup barbeque sauce
1/4 pound hickory wood chips, baste-soaked

TO PREPARE HICKORY TERIYAKI BASTE-MARINADE
1/2 cup finely chopped scallions (green onions)
1/2 cup finely chopped celery
1/2 cup (4 ounces) pure hickory liquid smoke
1/4 cup soy sauce
1/2 cup dry red wine
1 teaspoon liquid garlic (or mince 1 garlic clove)
1/2 cup fresh lemon juice, seeded and strained
2 cups water

In a 4-quart pot, combine all baste-marinade ingredients with the water on high heat. Reduce heat to medium, stir and simmer for 20 minutes, covered. Remove from heat.

TO MARINATE FLANK STEAKS
In a bowl or a sturdy plastic bag set in a rimmed container, pour half of baste-marinade over steaks and mushrooms. Cover bowl or twist-tie bag. Marinate 3 hours at room temperature or refrigerate overnight. Turn occasionally for thorough marinating.

PIT FIRE
Presoak hickory wood chips in 1 cup of baste-marinade for 10 minutes and drain. Spread soaked chips over close bed of 40-odd white-ash-hot charcoal briquets. Let chips burn into fire until flames are out (add more charcoal and soaked chips as needed).

PIT BASTING
When pit fire is ready, remove steaks from marinade. (Retain leftover marinade for pit-basting.) Place mushrooms and 1/2 cup of baste-marinade in thin aluminum pan on pit grill the last 20 minutes of total cooking time. Place steaks on lightly greased pit grill 4 to 6 inches above white-ash-hot fire. Cooking quickly, brown and brush-baste liberally each side, then turn and baste every 3 minutes for a total 12 to 15 minutes or until done the way you like flank steak. Brush on each side one coat of barbeque sauce for

another 2 minutes of cooking. When serving, slice steak across grain. Serve immediately with mushrooms and remaining sauce.

Makes 4 to 6 servings

HICKORY SMOKED BARBEQUE PORK

 ## Uncle Tom's Hickory Smoked "Bobby-Qued" Ribs

Over the years I have found that the most popular meat entree *treat* and delicacy is none other than pit-smoked barbeque spareribs — particularly ribs smoked with hickory wood. I offer here what I have perfected and what thousands have praised as one of the best backyard, picnic, pit grill recipe-methods for ribs that they've ever tasted.

    4 to 5 slabs (10 to 15 pounds) pork spareribs, cracked
    2 quarts Uncle Tom's Baste-Marinade (page 14)
    1¾ quarts of Bobby's Spicy Barbeque Sauce (page 22)
    1 tablespoon (approximately) *each* ground black pepper,
        garlic parsley salt, onion powder or onion parsley
        salt, paprika, celery seed (from shakers)
    1 pound of hickory wood chips, baste-soaked

TO MARINATE RIBS

With a meat cleaver, crack thick gristle bone in 4 to 5 places on each slab of ribs. Place slabs (whole or halved) in a sizable aluminum roasting pan or use a sturdy plastic bag set in a rimmed pan. Pour in approximately 1 quart of baste-marinade to submerge ribs. Cover pan or twist-tie plastic bag, pulling in close to submerge the ribs. Marinate for 3 hours at room temperature, turning occasionally, or refrigerate overnight. A 24-hour re-frigerated marinating gives excellent results. If using an aluminum pan, a hot, 200-degree, 30-minute marinating just before barbequing is also excellent.

PIT FIRE

Presoak hickory wood chips in 2 to 3 cups of baste-marinade for 30 minutes and let chips drain slightly before they are used. Spread half of soaked chips over a closed bed of 60 to 80 white-ash-hot charcoal briquets. Let wood chips burn into pit fire until flames are out. Midway through 3 hour cooking time spread second half of chips over an additional 30-odd white-ash-hot briquets. When ribs are placed on grill close cover and adjust pit damper vents three-fourths open.

SEAR SEASONING

As pit fire gets ready remove ribs from marinade and drain. (Retain used marinade and strain through a fine sieve for spraybasting over pit.) From shakers, sprinkle light coats of black pepper, garlic parsley salt, onion powder or onion parsley salt, paprika, and celery seed on both sides of ribs. With fingers and hands press and rub seasonings into meat. Place ribs on lightly greased grill 4 to 6 inches above hot pit fire. Sear and brown, seal in coated seasonings for 3 to 5 minutes on each side. For complete searing, rearrange slabs as they brown and close pit cover after turning.

PIT BASTING

Liberally brush or spray-baste browned ribs and turn and baste again every 10 to 15 minutes for 3 hours. Close cover after each basting. To control any pit flames lightly spray douse them with baste or water and/or adjust damper vents three-fourths closed for a couple of minutes. Constant basting over a pit fire kept at 250 to 300 degrees is necessary for juicy, tender, moist hickory-smoked spareribs.

SAUCING

During last 20 to 30 minutes of cooking time brush on sauce or tong-dip cut ribs in sauce every 10 minutes (close pit cover after each saucing), or brush sauce on whole slabs every 10 minutes, then cut into single pieces. Serve with heated sauce.

Makes 7 to 12 servings

Broiler-Oven "Bobby-Qued" Spareribs

When the harsh elements of winter prevent your firing up the outdoor pit grill and a craving for some righteous down-home hickory wood-smoked barbeque ribs manifests itself in a "Bobby-que" attack, the most immediate satisfaction that I can offer is the following ovenbroiler saucy hickory-smoke version of Bobby-que spareribs.

    2 or 3 slabs (6 to 9 pounds) pork spareribs
    2 quarts Uncle Tom's Baste-Marinade (page 14, make
        exactly half of recipe).
    Pan sauce (recipe follows)
    1 teaspoon *each* ground black pepper, garlic parsley salt,
        seasoning salt, onion powder, paprika, celery seed
        (from shakers)

TO PREPARE PAN SAUCE
    2 cups Uncle Tom's Baste-Marinade
    1 cup (eight ounce) tomato paste
    1/2 cup honey or 3/4 cup packed brown sugar or molasses
    1/4 cup spicy brown prepared mustard
    1/2 cup fresh lemon juice, seeded
    2 tablespoons dry crushed red pepper (or to taste)
    1/4 cup Tabasco sauce (or to taste)

Combine all ingredients in a 2-quart pot on medium heat. Stir and then simmer for 5 to 7 minutes. Put aside until ribs are half done.
Yields approximately 1 quart

BROILER SEAR SEASONING
Preheat broiler to 450 degrees (oven temperature the same). Cut rib slabs in 2- or 3 rib pieces. From shakers, sprinkle light coats of black pepper, garlic parsley salt, seasoning salt, onion powder, paprika, and celery seed on both sides of ribs. Thoroughly press seasonings into meat with fingers and hands. In a long baking pan, place ribs 4 to 6 inches below broiler heat. Sear, brown, and seal in coated seasonings for 3 to 5 minutes on each side, rearranging rib pieces so as not to burn already browned pieces until all rib pieces (and sides) are browned. Sprinkle a few drops of hickory liquid smoke on all browned rib pieces. Remove from broiler and drain fat from pan.

OVEN BASTING AND PAN SAUCING

Reduce oven heat to 375 degrees. Pour 3 cups of baste-marinade over ribs and place pan in oven. Bake uncovered for 30 minutes. Pour pan sauce over ribs, stirring sauce in pan. Baste ribs with pan sauce and bake for another 30 minutes tightly covered. Remove cover and bake another 15 minutes uncovered, basting ribs with pan sauce and rearranging ribs from bottom to top every 5 minutes to brown in sauce. Total cooking time is 75 minutes. If cooked longer for meat to begin to fall off the bone, cook covered.

Makes 6 to 10 servings

Hickory Lemon-Orange-Sherry Country-Style Ribs

8 pounds country-style pork ribs, cut approximately
    3/4-inch thick
2 quarts Lemon-Orange Baste-Marinade (recipe follows)
1 teaspoon (approximately) *each* garlic parsley salt,
    lemon pepper seasoning, seasoning salt (from
    shakers)
1/2 pound hickory wood chips, baste-soaked

TO PREPARE LEMON-ORANGE-SHERRY BASTE-MARINADE

Vegetables

1 cup *each* onions, scallions, celery, bell pepper, chopped
Cut rinds from 3 medium-size oranges and 4 lemons (hold
    juices for liquid ingredients)

Staples

1 tablespoon ground orange peel (from shaker)
1 teaspoon ground cloves
1 tablespoon lemon pepper seasoning

Liquids

1 1/2 cups fresh orange juice, seeded
1 cup fresh lemon juice, seeded
1 cup pineapple juice
1/4 cup cider vinegar
1 cup (8 ounces) pure hickory liquid smoke
1 quart water

Combine vegetable and staple ingredients in water in a 4-quart pot on high heat. Bring to a boil and reduce heat to medium. Stew for 30 minutes, covered. Remove from heat. Strain off stewed ingredients from liquid and add liquid ingredients, stirring thoroughly. Simmer on medium-low heat for 5 minutes. Remove from heat and let cool. Refrigerate overnight.

Yields approximately 2 quarts

TO MARINATE RIBS

In a tight-fitting container or a plastic bag set in a rimmed container, pour ¾ quart of baste-marinade over ribs. Cover container or twist-tie plastic bag. Marinate at room temperature for 2 hours or refrigerate overnight.

PIT FIRE

Presoak hickory wood chips in 2 cups of baste-marinade for 30 minutes and drain. Spread half of soaked chips over a close bed of 60-odd white-ash-hot charcoal briquets. Midway through cooking time, add more briquets as needed and second half of soaked chips. Damper vents should be three-fourths open.

SEAR SEASONING

When pit is ready, remove ribs from marinade and drain. (Retain used marinade for spray- or brush-basting over pit.) From shakers, sprinkle light coats of garlic parsley salt, lemon pepper seasoning, and seasoning salt on both sides. Press seasoning into meat with fingers and hands. Place ribs on lightly greased grill 4 to 6 inches above pit fire. Sear, brown, and seal in coated seasoning for 2 to 3 minutes on each side.

PIT BASTING

Spray-baste, brush-baste, or fork dip ribs in baste-marinade. Turn and baste every 10 to 15 minutes (pit top down after each basting) for 60 to 70 minutes. Brush on or tong-dip ribs in Apple-Lime-Mint barbeque sauce (page 25) every 5 minutes during last 20 minutes of cooking time.

Makes 8 to 10 servings.

Sweet and Sour Hickory-Qued Pork Chops

8 to 12 center-cut pork loin chops (approximately 5 to 7 pounds), cut thick
1½ quarts Sweet and Sour Hickory Baste-Marinade (recipe follows)

1 quart Sweet and Sour Hickory Sauce (recipe follows)
½ pound hickory wood chips, baste-soaked

TO PREPARE SWEET AND SOUR HICKORY BASTE-MARINADE
½ cup red wine vinegar
½ cup (4 ounces) pure hickory liquid smoke
¼ cup Worcestershire sauce
¼ cup dry sherry wine
¾ cup lemon juice, seeded
1 tablespoon liquid garlic (optional)
1 cup apricot nectar
1 cup pineapple juice
3 cups water

Combine baste-marinade ingredients with water in a 4-quart pot on high heat. Stir and bring to a quick boil. Remove from heat.
Yields 1¾ quart

TO PREPARE SWEET AND SOUR HICKORY SAUCE
½ cup *each* finely chopped onions, finely chopped celery,
    grated carrot (to be pureed with other ingredients)
2 tablespoons prepared mustard (substitute spicy hot
    mustard if desired)
3 dripping tablespoons honey or 3 heaping tablespoons
    brown sugar
½ cup fresh lemon juice, seeded
2 cups V-8 juice or puree 16-ounce can stewed tomatoes,
    pureed
1½ cups Sweet and Sour Hickory Baste-Marinade*

Combine all ingredients. Add pureed ingredients, except for baste, in a blender and puree. Combine pureed ingredients to another ¾ cups Sweet and Sour Hickory Baste-Marinade in a 4-quart pot on high heat. Stir thoroughly and bring to a boil. Reduce heat to medium low. Let simmer, covered, for 20 minutes or until it thickens. Remove from heat.
Yields approximately 1 quart

TO MARINATE CHOPS
Place pork chops in a close-fitting container or in a plastic bag set in a rimmed container. Pour 2 to 3 cups of baste-marinade over chops. Cover

---

Use 3/4 cup of baste-marinade to rinse blender.

container or twist-tie plastic bag. Marinate at room temperature for 2 hours or refrigerate overnight. Turn occasionally for thorough marinating.

PIT FIRE

Presoak hickory wood chips in 1 cup of baste-marinade for 20 minutes and drain. Spread soaked chips evenly over a close bed of 50-odd white-ash-hot charcoal briquets. Let chips burn into fire until flames are out. Adjust dampers half open.

PIT BASTING

When pit fire is ready, remove chops from marinade and drain. (Retain used marinade for pit-basting.) Place chops on lightly greased pit grill 4 to 6 inches above pit fire. Spray- or brush-baste, browning, then turn and baste every 5 minutes (pit cover down after each basting) for 30 minutes or until done the way you like pork chops. Tong-dip chops in Sweet and Sour Hickory Sauce twice during last 5 minutes of cooking time. Serve immediately with remaining sauce.

Makes 4 to 6 servings

Pit-Smoked Pork Shoulder Roast

6- to 10-pound pork shoulder roast
1 teaspoon (approximately) *each* of seasoning salt, black pepper, garlic parsley salt, fine ground cloves (from shakers)
2 quarts Uncle Tom's Baste-Marinade (page 14, make exactly half of recipe)
Several slivers each of garlic, onion, bell pepper, onion
½ pound hickory wood chips, baste-soaked

TO MARINATE PORK ROAST

With a sharp knife poke several holes 1 to 1½ inches deep into lean meat of roast. Press garlic, onion and bell pepper slivers into holes. Place roast in a close-fitting container or in a sturdy plastic bag set in a rimmed container. Pour in approximately 3 cups baste-marinade to submerge roast. Cover container or twist-tie plastic bag, pulling in close to submerge the meat. Marinate for 3 hours at room temperature or refrigerate overnight. Twenty-four hours in the refrigerator gives excellent results. Turn occasionally for thorough marinating.

PIT FIRE

Presoak hickory wood chips in 1½ cups of baste-marinade for 30 minutes and drain. Evenly spread half of soaked chips over a close bed of 50-odd white-ash-hot charcoal briquets. Let chips burn into pit fire until flames are out. Add more briquets as needed and second half of soaked chips midway through cooking time. For continuous hickory smoke, leave damper vents half open. Pit temperature should be between 250 and 300 degrees.

SEAR SEASONING

When pit fire is ready, remove roast from marinade and drain. (Retain used marinade for pit-basting, straining it through fine sieve if using spray-basting. From shakers, sprinkle light coats of seasoning salt, black pepper, garlic parsley salt, and ground cloves all over roast, pressing and rubbing in seasonings with fingers and hands. Place roast on pit grill 4 to 6 inches above hot pit fire. Sear meat and seal in coated seasoning for 3 to 5 minutes, browning all sides of roast

PIT BASTING

Place roast in a sizable 1-inch-rimmed aluminum pan in center of grill. Baste and turn every 20 minutes for 3 to 4 hours, adding charcoal briquets and soaked chips to maintain steady smoke and 275-degree pit temperature. Cook until roast is done to your liking. Slice and serve with desired barbeque sauce.

Makes 6 to 12 servings

Pit-Glazed Hickory-Pineapple Ham Steaks

4 to 6 center-cut ham slices, cut ½ inch thick
1 quart Saucy Hickory Pineapple Marinade (recipe
    follows)
½ pound of hickory wood chips (baste-soaked)

TO PREPARE SAUCY HICKORY PINEAPPLE MARINADE
½ cup (4 ounces) pure hickory liquid smoke
¾ cup dry sherry wine
1½ cups pineapple juice
¼ cup Worcestershire sauce
¼ cup red wine vinegar
2 cups V-8 juice or 1 16-ounce can stewed tomatoes

½ cup of packed brown sugar or ½ cup honey
1 tablespoon spicy hot brown prepared mustard
½ cube butter or margarine
½ teaspoon ground cloves
3 cups water

Combine liquid smoke, sherry, pineapple juice, Worcestershire sauce and vinegar with the 3 cups of water in a 3-quart pot on high heat. Stir and bring to a quick boil. Remove from heat. Separate out 2 cups for soaking the hickory wood chips. To the remaining 2 cups add the rest of the ingredients.

2 cups V-8 juice (or puree 16 oz. can of stewed tomatoes)
½ cup of brown sugar (or honey)
1 tablespoon spicy hot brown mustard
½ cube of butter or margarine
½ teaspoon ground cloves

Stir thoroughly and let simmer, covered, for 20 minutes on medium-low heat Remove from heat and let cool, or refrigerate overnight.

Yields approximately 1 quart

TO MARINATE HAM STEAKS

Cut 1 or 2 slashes in any fat edges to keep meat from curling on pit grill. Place ham steaks in a sizable tight-fitting container or use a sturdy plastic bag set in a rimmed container. Pour saucy marinade over steaks. Marinate for 1 hour at room temperature, covered. Rearrange steaks in container or turn in plastic bag for thorough marinating.

PIT FIRE

Presoak hickory wood chips in reserved baste-marinade for 20 minutes and drain. Evenly spread soaked chips over a close bed of 50-odd white-ash-hot charcoal briquets. Let chips burn into fire until flames.

PIT BASTING

When pit fire is ready, remove ham steaks from Saucy Hickory Pineapple Marinade and drain slightly. (Retain used marinade for pit brush-basting). Place steaks on lightly greased grill 4 to 6 inches above hot pit fire. Brush-baste with sauce, turn and baste again (pit cover down after each basting) every 3 to 5 minutes for 15 minutes. Remove from heat and serve immediately with remaining sauce, heated.

Makes 4 to 6 servings

Hickory-Smoked Country Rib Roast

4- to 6-pounds pork country rib roast
2 quarts Uncle Tom's Baste-Marinade (page 14)
¾ quart of barbeque sauce desired (pages 22 to 25)
1 teaspoon approximately each of garlic parsley salt,
    onion powder, ground clove, celery salt
½ pound (plus) hickory wood chips (baste-soaked)

TO MARINATE COUNTRY RIB ROAST

Place roast in a close-fitting container or in a sturdy plastic bag set in a rimmed container. Pour ½ to ¾ quarts of baste-marinade over roast, submerging meat. Cover container or twist-tie plastic bag, pulling in close for thorough marinating. Marinate for 3 hours at room temperature or refrigerate overnight; 24 hours in the refrigerator is excellent. Turn occasionally for thorough marinating.

PIT FIRE

Presoak hickory wood chips in 2 cups of baste-marinade for 30 minutes and drain. Evenly spread half of the soaked chips over a close bed of 60-odd white-ash-hot charcoal briquets. Let chips burn into pit fire until flames are out. Add 10 to 20 more briquets as needed and second half of soaked chips midway through cooking time. Adjust damper vents three-fourths closed at first, then three-fourths open midway through cooking time.

SEAR SEASONING

When pit fire is ready, remove country rib roast from marinade and drain. (Retain used marinade and strain it through a fine sieve for spray-basting over pit later.) From shakers, sprinkle light coats of garlic parsley salt, onion powder, ground clove, and celery salt on all sides of roast. With fingers and hands press and rub in seasonings. Place roast on pit grill 4 to 6 inches above hot pit fire. Sear meat and seal in coated seasoning for 3 to 5 minutes, browning all sides. Pit cover should be down.

PIT BASTING

After sear seasoning place roast in a sizable, thin, 1-inch-rimmed, throwaway aluminum pan in center of pit grill. Liberally spray-baste or brush baste, turning and basting every 20 to 30 minutes for 3 hours or until meat is done in the center. Fork or tong-dip roast into pot of warm barbeque sauce or brush on sauce 2 or 3 times during last 20 minutes of cooking time. When saucing, remove aluminum pan and place roast directly over pit fire pan for a glazed exterior and deep saucy taste. Slice servings between each rib. Serve immediately with remaining sauce.

Makes 4 to 8 servings

HICKORY-SMOKED BARBEQUE LAMB

Hickory-Smoked Garlic Mint Butterflied Leg of Lamb

1 leg of lamb (10 to 12 pounds), deboned and butterflied
2 quarts *Lime-Mint Garlic-Onion Baste-Marinade (page 17)*
1 teaspoon *each* garlic parsley salt, black pepper,
    seasoning salt (from shakers)
1 pound hickory wood chips, baste-soaked

TO MARINATE LEG OF LAMB

Place butterflied leg of lamb in a sturdy plastic bag set in a rimmed pan. Pour half of baste-marinade (about a quart) over lamb. Twist-tie bag shut, pulling close in to submerge lamb in marinade. Turn occasionally for thorough marinating. Marinate for 2 hours at room temperature or refrigerate overnight.

PIT FIRE

Presoak the hickory wood chips in 2 cups of baste-marinade for 30 minutes and drain. Spread half of soaked chips over a solid bed of 60-odd white-ash-hot charcoal briquets. Let chips burn into fire until flames are out. Add remaining soaked chips midway through total cooking time.

SEAR SEASONING

When pit fire is ready, remove leg of lamb from marinade and drain. (Retain used marinade and strain through a fine sieve for pit spray-basting later.) From shakers, sprinkle medium coats of garlic parsley salt, black pepper, and ground seasoning on all sides of butterflied leg of lamb. With fingers and hands, thoroughly rub and press seasoning into meat. Place leg of lamb on lightly greased pit grill 4 to 6 inches above pit fire. Sear and seal in the seasoning for 3 to 5 minutes, browning meat on all sides.

PIT BASTING

Turn and brush- or spray-baste leg of lamb every 10 to 15 minutes for a period of 60 minutes for a pink center, or cook longer, basting regularly until done the way you like lamb (be sure to cover pit after each basting). Damper vents should be adjusted ¾ closed. Serve with sauce desired.

Makes 8 to 10 servings

Hickory-Qued Lamb Steaks

6 lamb steaks from large end leg of lamb cut ¾ to 1 inch
    thick
¾ quart Hickory Garlic-Lime-Mint Baste-Marinade (recipe
    follows)
1 teaspoon (approximately) *each* lemon pepper
    seasoning, seasoning salt (from shakers)
½ pound hickory wood chips baste-soaked

TO PREPARE HICKORY GARLIC-LIME-MINT BASTE-MARINADE

⅓ cube butter or margarine
½ cup chopped onion-garlic (if unavailable substitute
1 tablespoon *each* liquid garlic and onion juice)
½ cup (4 ounces) pure hickory liquid smoke
½ cup dry red wine
½ cup red wine vinegar
¼ cup liquid mint or 7 or 8 fresh whole mint leaves
¾ cup finely chopped green onions (use some green tops)
½ cup finely chopped bell pepper
Juice of 4 limes seeded (cup up rinds and include in pot)
1 teaspoon *each* lemon pepper seasoning, garlic parsley
    salt
¾ quart water

Set aside butter or margarine. Combine all other baste ingredients with the water in a 3-quart pot on high heat. Bring to a boil. Reduce heat to medium and simmer for 20 minutes, covered. Remove from heat and let cool a bit. Strain off stewed vegetables and rinds from liquid and separate out 1 cup of baste to soak hickory wood chips. Stir melted butter or margarine into remaining warm or heated baste.

TO MARINATE LAMB STEAKS

In a tight-fitting container or a sturdy plastic bag set in a rimmed pan, pour baste-marinade over lamb steaks. Twist-tie plastic bag or cover container. Marinate, refrigerated, for 4 hours or until next day. Turn occasionally for thorough marinating.

PIT FIRE

Presoak hickory wood chips in 1 cup of baste-marinade for 30 minutes and drain. Spread soaked chips over a close bed of 40-odd white-ash-hot charcoal briquets. Let chips burn into fire until flames are out.

SEAR SEASONING

When pit fire is ready, remove steaks from marinade and drain. (Retain used marinade for pit-basting.) From shakers, sprinkle light coats of lemon pepper seasoning and seasoning salt on both sides of steaks. With fingers and hands, press seasoning into meat. Place steaks on lightly greased grill 4 to 6 inches above hot pit fire. Sear, brown 2 to 3 minutes on each side, sealing in coated seasoning.

PIT BASTING

Liberally spray- or brush-baste steaks, then turn and baste again every 5 minutes (shutting pit cover after each basting) for 20 minutes for a pink center or until done the way you like lamb steaks. Serve immediately with your choice of barbeque sauce (if desired).

Makes 6 Servings

Hickory-Qued Fruit Sauce Lamb Kabobs

2½ pounds lean boneless lamb (leg or shoulder), cut into
    1¾ inch cubes
¾ quart Fruit Sauce-Lamb Marinade (recipe follows)
½ pound medium-size mushrooms, left whole
2 large bell peppers, seeded and cut in 1¾ inch squares
1 teaspoon (approximately) lemon-pepper seasoning
    seasoning salt (from shakers)
¼ pound hickory wood chips water-soaked

TO PREPARE FRUIT SAUCE-MARINADE FOR LAMB

½ cup *each* cranberry juice and grape juice
½ cup apple juice or pineapple juice
½ cup dry sherry
¼ cup pure hickory liquid smoke
¼ cup red wine vinegar
¼ cup fresh lemon juice, seeded
1 cup V-8 juice
¼ cup Worcestershire sauce
1 tablespoon *each* liquid garlic-onion juice, lemon pepper
    seasoning, seasoning salt
¼ cube butter or margarine

Combine all marinade ingredients in a 2-quart pot on medium heat. Simmer for 15 minutes uncovered or until slight thickening occurs, stirring occasionally. Set aside and let cool.

Yields approximately 1 quart

TO MARINATE MEAT

In a sizable bowl or a plastic bag set in a rimmed pan, pour marinade over cubed lamb pieces. Add mushrooms and bell pepper squares. Cover bowl or twist-tie plastic bag. Marinate, refrigerated, for 3 hours or overnight.

PIT FIRE

Presoak hickory wood chips in water for 30 minutes and drain. Spread soaked chips over a close bed of 40-odd white-ash-hot charcoal briquets. Let chips burn into pit fire until flames are out.

PIT BASTING

When pit fire is ready, remove lamb cubes, mushrooms, and bell pepper squares from marinade and drain. (Retain used marinade for pit-basting.) Sprinkle light coats of lemon pepper seasoning and seasoning salt from shakers over lamb-qued pieces. Using 6 sturdy metal skewers, alternate meat, bell pepper, meat, mushrooms etc. equally dividing the meat and vegetables among the skewers. Place kabobs on a lightly greased grill 4 to 6 inches above pit fire. Baste with fruit sauce, turning kabobs, liberally basting every 3 to 5 minutes (cover top down after basting) for 10 to 20 minutes or until done the way you like them. Serve with remaining fruit sauce.

Makes 6 servings

HICKORY-SMOKED BARBEQUE POULTRY

Saucy Pit-Qued Chicken

If you don't want to fire up the pit, you can make this saucy chicken in the broiler-oven.

> 3, 4, 5 fryerbroiler chickens (3 to 3½ pounds each) cut in
>   quarters
> 3 quarts Uncle Tom's Bobby-Que Baste-Marinade (page
>   14)
> 1 tablespoon (approximately) *each*, seasoning salt, onion
>   parsley salt, ground black pepper, paprika (from
>   shakers)
> ½ cube butter or margarine (hold for strained marinade)
> 4 cups Hickory Chicken Sauce (recipe follows)
> ½ pound hickory wood chips baste-soaked

TO PREPARE HICKORY CHICKEN SAUCE
> 3 cups V-8 juice
> ⅓ cup (3 ounces) pure hickory liquid smoke
> ⅓ cup Worcestershire sauce
> 1 teaspoon chicken bouillon
> 1 tablespoon prepared mustard
> 2 tablespoon packed brown sugar or 2 dripping
>   tablespoons honey
> ⅓ cup fresh lemon juice, seeded
> 1½ cup Uncle Tom's Baste-Marinade

Combine all sauce ingredients with Uncle Tom's Baste-Marinade in a 3-quart pot. Stir thoroughly and boil gently for 30 minutes, covered, stirring periodically. Remove from heat with a final stir.

Yields approx. 1¼ quarts. If barbequing 5 chickens add extra cup of baste-marinade to stretch.

TO MARINATE CHICKEN

Rinse quartered chicken parts and remove any excessive fatty hangings. Place chicken in sizable container(s) or use sturdy plastic bag(s) set in a rimmed container. Pour in 1½ quarts of cooled Uncle Tom's Bobby-Que Baste-Marinade, submerging all chicken quarters. Arrange chicken so that marinade soaks all parts thoroughly. Cover container(s) or twist-tie plastic bag(s). Marinate for 2 to 3 hours at room temperature or refrigerate overnight.

PIT FIRE

Presoak hickory wood chips in 2 cups of baste-marinade for 30 minutes and drain. Evenly spread half of soaked chips over a close bed of 50 to 60 white-ash-hot charcoal briquets. Let chips burn into pit fire until flames are out. Spread remaining half of soaked chips over briquets midway through cooking time.

SEAR SEASONING

When pit fire is ready, remove chicken quarters from marinade and thoroughly drain. Retain used marinade, strain it through a fine sieve, heat it, and stir in the butter or margarine for pit-basting. From shakers, sprinkle light coats of seasoning salt, onion parsley salt, black pepper, and paprika on both sides of chicken quarters. With fingers and hands press and rub seasonings into meat. Place chicken on lightly greased grill 4 to 6 inches above pit fire. Sear, brown, and seal in coated seasonings for 3 to 5 minutes on each side, alternating quarters placed on top of others. (Using a kettle pit grill with a 22-inch-diameter cover, you can always pile chicken quarters or halves on top of one another.) Keep pit cover on, adjusting dampers half open to keep flames down.

PIT BASTING

Liberally spray or brush-baste browned chicken quarters or tong-dip them in baste, then turn and baste every 10 minutes (pit cover down after each basting) for 50-60 minutes or until done the way you like chicken. (Chicken is done when meat near bone is no longer pink.) Brush on Hickory Chicken Sauce 2 to 3 times on each side (or tong-dip quarters in sauce pot) every 5 minutes during last 15 minutes of cooking time. Serve with remaining Hickory Chicken Sauce.

Makes 10 to 15 servings

BROILER-OVEN METHOD (FOR 3 CHICKENS)

Preheat oven broiler (oven the same) to 400 degrees. Place marinated chicken pieces coated with seasonings in a sizable rectangular pan 4 to 6 inches below broiler heat. Broil, rearranging chicken occasionally to brown all pieces, for approximately 20 minutes. Bake in oven, covered, for 40 more minutes, basting every 15 minutes (add 1 or 2 cups of baste-marinade in bottom of pan as needed for moisture), or bake 5 to 10 minutes until meat is no longer pink near bone when forked. Brush on Hickory Chicken Sauce or tong-dip pieces in sauce, cover pan and bake for another 15 to 20 minutes. Total cooking time, including broiling time, approximately 75 minutes. Serve immediately with remaining, heated Hickory Chicken Sauce.

Makes 8 to 10 servings

Hickory-Smoked Turkey Parts

6 to 10 turkey wings, thighs or legs or combination of
    wings, thighs, and legs
1½ quarts Hickory-Quick Barbeque Baste-Marinade (page
    20)
Hickory Chicken Sauce (page 61)
½ cube butter or margarine, melted
½ pound hickory wood chips, baste-soaked

TO MARINATE TURKEY PARTS

Reserve 2 cups of Hickory-Quick Barbeque sauce for soaking hickory wood chips. Combine remaining sauce with melted butter or margarine to make a baste-marinade. Place turkey parts in a tight-fitting container or use a sturdy plastic bag set in a rimmed pan. Pour 3 to 4 cups of baste-marinade over turkey, submerging the parts. Cover container or twist-tie plastic bag. Marinate for 3 hours at room temperature or refrigerate overnight. Turn occasionally for thorough marinating.

PIT FIRE

Presoak hickory wood chips in the reserved Hickory-Quick Barbeque Sauce for 20 minutes and drain. Spread half of soaked chips over a close bed of 60-odd white-ash-hot charcoal briquets. Let chips burn into the pit fire until flames are out. Add 8 to 10 charcoal briquets after 35 minutes of cooking time and spread remaining soaked chips over hot bed of coals. (See damper vent adjustments under pit basting.)

PIT BASTING

Remove turkey parts from baste-marinade and drain. Retain and strain used baste for pit spray-basting. Place turkey on lightly greased grill 4 to 6 inches above pit fire. Brush or spraybaste turkey parts frequently, turning every 10 minutes (pit cover down) for 30 minutes until golden brown. Barbeque, keep damper vents ¾ open, basting and turning every 10 to 15 minutes for another 70 minutes or cook until meat is no longer pink near bone when forked. Serve with Hickory Chicken Sauce.

Makes 6 to 10 servings

Hickory Smoked Cornish Hens
(with Wild Rice Goober Stuffing)

   4 Cornish hens (about 1¼ pounds each), thawed
   1½ quarts Hickory Herbal Butter Baste-Marinade (recipe
       follows)
   1 quart Wild Rice and Goober* Stuffing (recipe follows)
   1½ quarts Hickory Chicken Sauce (optional, page 61)
   ⅓ pound hickory wood chips, baste-soaked

TO PREPARE HICKORY HERBAL BUTTER BASTE-MARINADE
Vegetables
   ½ cup *each* finely chopped green onions, finely chopped
       celery, grated carrots, finely chopped red or green
       bell peppers
   1 clove minced garlic

Staples
   1 teaspoon *each* black pepper, garlic parsley salt, onion
       powder
   2 tablespoons blended herbs (should include sage,
       thyme, marjoram, basil, bay leaves)

Liquids
   ½ cup (4 ounces) pure hickory liquid smoke
   ¼ cup fresh lemon juice, seeded

We're using the generic African meaning for "nuts" and not referring to peanuts.

½ cup red wine vinegar
1 cup dry white cooking wine
½ cube butter or margarine
2 cups cranberry juice
5 cups water

Combine vegetable and staple ingredients with water in a 4-quart pot on high heat. Stir, bring to a boil, and reduce heat to medium. Boil gently for 30 minutes, covered. Remove from heat. With a fine wire strainer, separate stewed vegetables and reserve for stuffing. Stir liquid smoke, lemon juice, vinegar, and cooking wine into *hot* baste-marinade. (At this point separate out 2 cups of baste for soaking hickory wood chips.) Add butter or margarine and cranberry juice to remaining marinade, stirring thoroughly. Simmer for 5 minutes on low heat, covered. Set aside and let cool.

Yields approximately 2 quarts

TO PREPARE WILD RICE AND GOOBER STUFFING
1½ cup *cooked* wild rice (recipe follow)
¾ cup chopped black walnuts
1 cup seasoned stuffing mix (or use 3 or 4 slices of rye
    bread, diced)
½ cup *each* chopped green onions, chopped celery,
    chopped bell pepper, grated carrot
1 cup hot Hickory Herbal Butter Baste-Marinade
¼ teaspoon *each* black pepper, garlic parsley salt

To cook wild rice: Add ¾ cup of uncooked wild rice to 2 cups boiling water, ½ teaspoon onion salt, and 1 tablespoon butter or margarine. Reduce heat to low. Steam, covered, for 30 minutes (or until flaky). Set aside and let cool.

Lightly mix rice and other stuffing ingredients together and add hot baste-marinade. Mix thoroughly and stuff marinated hens.

TO MARINATE CORNISH HENS
Place thawed Cornish hens in tight-fitting container or in a sturdy plastic bag set in a rimmed pan. Pour all but 1 cup of baste-marinade over hens. Cover container or twist-tie plastic bag, pulling in close. Marinate for 2 hours at room temperature or refrigerate overnight. Turn occasionally for thorough marinating.

PIT FIRE
Presoak the hickory wood chips in 2 cups of baste-marinade reserved for this purpose. Let soak for 30 minutes and drain. Spread soaked chips

over a close bed of 40-odd white-ash-hot charcoal briquets. Let chips burn into fire until flames are out. Add 5 to 10 more briquets, as needed, midway through cooking time.

STUFFING AND PIT BASTING

When pit fire is ready, remove hens from marinade. (Retain and strain used marinade for pit spray- or brush-basting.) Stuff hens in body cavity and tie legs with string or cord. (Pan-bake any remaining stuffing on covered pit for 30 minutes or in oven for 20 minutes.)

Put hens in a large, thin throwaway aluminum pan (or use 2 aluminum pans) and place 4 to 6 inches above pit fire. Adjust damper vents half to three-fourths open. Brush- or spray-baste every 10 minutes for 60 to 70 minutes, closing pit cover after each basting.

SAUCING

If desired, brush on Hickory Chicken Sauce or tong-dip each hen in a pot of sauce 2 or 3 times during last 10 to 15 minutes of cooking time.

Makes 4 servings

Hickory Pit-Smoked Whole Turkey

You can stuff the bird or not, and if you want to there's a delectable corn bread stuffing to try.

    1 turkey (9 to 18 pounds)
    4 quarts Hickory Cranberry-Apple Baste-Marinade
        (recipe follows)
    3 quarts Goobered Corn Bread Stuffing (optional) (recipe
        follows)
    2 pounds hickory wood chips, baste-soaked

TO PREPARE HICKORY CRANBERRY-APPLE BASTE-MARINADE
Vegetables
    1 cup *each* chopped onions, chopped bell peppers,
        grated carrots, chopped celery
    2 cloves chopped garlic

Staples
    2 bay leaves
    1 teaspoon *each* black pepper, onion parsley salt, celery
        salt, poultry seasoning

1 teaspoon chicken bouillon extract

Liquids
    2 cups cranberry-apple juice
    3/4 cup (6 ounces) pure hickory liquid smoke
    1/2 cup red wine vinegar or red cooking wine
    1/2 cup fresh lemon juice, seeded
    4 quarts water
    1 cube (1/4 pound) butter or margarine

Combine vegetable and staple ingredients in water in a 6-quart pot on high heat. Bring to a boil. Remove from heat and let cool. Strain off stewed ingredients from liquid and add all liquid ingredients *except* butter or margarine. Simmer on medium-low heat for 10 minutes. Remove from heat.

Separate out 1/2 quart of baste for soaking hickory wood chips. To the rest, add butter or margarine and stir well.

Yield 5 quarts plus

TO MARINATE TURKEY

Place thawed turkey (including neck and giblets) in a sturdy sizable plastic bag set in a high-rimmed roasting pan. Depending on size of turkey, pour 1 to 2 quarts of baste-marinade over it. Twist-tie plastic bag, with marinade covering at least two-thirds of turkey's surface. Marinate 3 hours at room temperature or refrigerate overnight. Turn over occasionally to allow for thorough marinating. If refrigerated overnight, remove 1 hour before pit smoke cooking begins. (Remove giblets and neck early if preparing corn bread stuffing.)

PIT FIRE

Presoak the 2 pounds of hickory wood chips in 1/2 quart of baste-marinade for 30 minutes and drain as used. (Retain used baste as more soaked chips may be needed.) Bank 60 to 70 white-ash-hot charcoal briquets along two sides of lower pit charcoal grate (30 to 35 on each side).

Place drip pan in center of banked briquets. Spread one fourth pound of soaked chips over banked-white-ash-hot briquets. Place pit thermometer on pit grill (not lower grate). Adjust damper vents approximately three-fourths open to maintain temperature of 250 to 300 degrees. Add 20 charcoal briquets and 1/2 pound of soaked chips every 50 to 60 minutes of total cooking time.

TO STUFF TURKEY

When pit fire is ready, remove turkey from marinade and thoroughly drain. (Retain used marinade for pit basting.) If stuffing, prepare your favorite or use the *Goobered Corn Bread Stuffing* recipe that follows. Using about ⅔ cup stuffing per pound of turkey, fully stuff body cavity and neck cavity. Fasten neck skin and lace it closed with string or cord. Tie end of legs together and tie wings under body. If extra stuffing is left over, pan-bake on pit or in oven at 250-degrees for 35 to 40 minutes.

TO PREPARE GOOBERED* CORN BREAD STUFFING
    Half or all of giblets and neck (which have been boiled in
        3 cups baste-marinade for ½ hour, covered, on
        medium heat)
    1 pan corn bread, baked according to meal box recipe
        and crumbled
    7 or 8 slices rye or wheat bread, diced or crumbled
    ½ cup *each* chopped onions, chopped scallions, chopped
        celery, finely grated carrot
    3 hard-boiled eggs, chopped
    1 cup finely chopped walnuts
    2 cups baste-marinade taken from baste-marinade used
        to boil giblets
    ½ teaspoon *each* garlic parsley salt, onion salt, celery
        salt, black pepper (or season to taste from shakers)

Remove meat from turkey neck and chop up giblets. Combine neck meat, giblets, corn bread, rye or wheat bread, vegetables, and hard-boiled eggs in a 6-quart bowl. Mix thoroughly. Add nuts and baste-marinade, again mixing thoroughly. If desired, add a bit more for moister stuffing. Season with salts and pepper to taste. Mix thoroughly and stuff turkey.
Makes approximately 3 quarts

PIT BASTING
Place turkey directly on grill (after banking coals) or place turkey in a large round or oval aluminum throwaway pan 4 to 6 inches above pit fire. Average pit smoking time is 15 to 20 minutes per pound, or until a meat thermometer inserted into thickest portion (be sure it doesn't touch bone) registers 185 to 200 degrees. A turkey with a pop-up indicator is done when the indicator has fully risen. Liberally and completely brush or spray-baste turkey every 20 to 30 minutes during the entire cooking time for approximately 3 hours for a 9 to 12 pound bird.

Close pit cover after each basting and keep dampers adjusted approximately three-fourths open. (Remember to maintain pit fire by adding briquets and soaked chips as needed for constant 275 pit thermometer

---

Generic African meaning for "nut," not peanut.

temperature. For larger birds (15 to 18 pounds), remove turkey from pit after four hours and bake in oven at for another hour, covered with aluminum foil, until done. After removing turkey from pit or oven, let stand for 15 minutes before carving.

Hickory-Smoked Fried Chicken

I came about this recipe quite by accident. One day while my family and I were barbequing chicken, it suddenly started to pour down rain. My wife and I rushed to remove the half-done chicken from the pit and hurriedly took it inside the house. It was very hot and humid that summer day so we didn't want to broil or bake it (turning the oven on would have made the house unbearably hot). We decided to coat the chicken with cornmeal and flour and fry it. To our surprise, the already pit-qued hickory-smoked flavor created a delectable treat which I share with you in the following recipe.

    2 3-pound chickens cut in eighths
    1 quart Hickory-Quick Onion Baste-Marinade (recipe
        follows)
    1 tablespoon seasoning salt (from shaker)
    1½ to 2 cups pure vegetable oil
    ¼ cube butter or margarine
    ½ cup corn meal and 1½ cups flour, blended together
    ¼ pound hickory wood chips, baste-soaked

TO PREPARE HICKORY-QUICK ONION BASTE-MARINADE
    ⅓ cup (3 ounces) pure hickory liquid smoke
    ½ cup red wine vinegar or cider vinegar
    ½ cup fresh lemon juice, seeded
    1 tablespoon onion powder
    ½ cup Worcestershire sauce
    3 cups water

Combine all ingredients with water in a 3-quart pot on high heat. Stir and bring to a boil. Remove from heat.
    Makes 1 quart plus

TO MARINATE CHICKEN
    Place chicken pieces in a sizable bowl or pot. Pour enough baste-marinade over chicken pieces to cover (about 3 cups), and arrange pieces for

thorough marinating with hot marinade, leave for ½ hour at room temperature.

PIT FIRE

Presoak hickory wood chips in 1 cup of baste-marinade for 30 minutes and drain. Spread chips over 20 to 30 white-ash-hot charcoal briquets. Let chips burn into fire until flames are out.

ON THE PIT

Remove chicken from marinade and drain. (Retain used marinade and strain through a fine sieve for pit basting.) From shaker, sprinkle a light coat of seasoning salt all over chicken pieces. Place on pit grill 4 to 6 inches from heat. Keep pit cover down after basting twice and turning. After 20 to 25 minutes, remove half-done smoked chicken from pit.

IN THE PAN

In a 3 or 4 quart frying pan, heat vegetable oil and butter or margarine over medium heat. Place chicken in bag containing blended corn meal and flour. Shake thoroughly to coat chicken. When oil and butter are hot, reduce heat to medium low. Place chicken in one layer in pan and fry covered for 7 to 10 minutes turning to brown on each side. Turn again and cook for another 15 to 20 minutes until done. Repeat frying procedure if using smaller-sized frying pan. Serve immediately.

Makes 8 servings

Smoked Spicy Hot Barbeque Chicken

2 fryerbroiler chickens, 3 to 3½ pounds each, cut in
    quarters or eighths)
1 quart Hickory-Quick Baste-Marinade (page 69)
3 cups Spicy Hot Chicken Sauce (recipe follows)
3 cups hickory wood chips, baste-soaked

TO PREPARE SPICY HOT CHICKEN SAUCE

3 cups V-8 juice
⅓ cup (3 ounces) pure hickory liquid smoke
⅓ cup Worcestershire sauce
1 tablespoon crushed red pepper
⅓ cup hot jalapeño peppers, finely chopped
1 cup Hickory-Quick Baste-Marinade

Combine all ingredients in a 4-quart pot. Stir thoroughly and boil gently for 25 minutes on medium heat, covered, stirring periodically. With a final stir remove from heat .

Yields approximately 1 quart

TO MARINATE CHICKEN

Place chicken pieces in sizable pot or bowl or use a plastic bag set in a rimmed container. Pour ½ quart of baste-marinade to submerge chicken. Cover pot or bowl or twist-tie plastic bag. Marinate for 2 hours at room temperature or refrigerate overnight. Turn occasionally for thorough marinating.

PIT FIRE

Presoak hickory wood chips in 1 cup of Hickory-Quick Baste-Marinade for 30 minutes and drain. Evenly spread soaked chips over a close bed of 40-odd white-ash-hot charcoal briquets. Let chips burn into pit fire until flames are out.

PIT BASTING

When pit fire is ready, remove chicken pieces from marinade and drain. (Retain used marinade and strain through a fine sieve for pit basting.) Place chicken pieces on lightly greased pit grill 4 to 6 inches above pit fire. Brush or spray-baste, browning and turning frequently for 50 minutes or until chicken is done the way you like it. Test to be sure the meat near bone is no longer pink when forked. Brush on Spicy Hot Hickory Chicken Sauce or tong-dip chicken pieces in sauce pot 2 or 3 times during last 10 minutes of cooking time. Serve with remaining sauce.

Makes 8 servings

BARBEQUED FISH

Hickory-Qued Salmon Steaks

6 salmon steaks (3 to 3½ pounds), cut ¾ inch thick
4 cups Hickory Butter Lime Baste-Marinade (recipe
    follows)
½ pound hickory wood chips, baste-soaked
Lemon pepper seasoning, seasoning salt (from shakers)

TO PREPARE HICKORY BUTTER LIME BASTE-MARINADE

⅓ cup (3 ounces) pure hickory liquid smoke
¼ cup fresh lime juice, seeded
½ cup dry sherry
½ cup red wine vinegar
1 tablespoon *each* liquid onion, liquid garlic
1 teaspoon *each* dry rosemary, crushed chives, lemon
    pepper seasoning, paprika, seasoning salt
½ cube butter or margarine
3 cups water

Set aside butter or margarine. Combine all other ingredients with water in a 2-quart pot on high heat. Stir and bring to a quick boil. Remove from heat. Strain and separate out 1½ cups to baste-soak hickory wood chips. Add butter or margarine to remaining hot baste-marinade, stirring to melt.

PIT FIRE

Presoak hickory wood chips in reserved baste for 20 minutes and drain. Spread soaked chips over a close bed of 30-odd white-ash-hot charcoal briquets. Let chips burn into pit fire until flames are out.

TO MARINATE SALMON STEAKS

Pour buttered marinade over steaks in a rimmed container, covering both sides. Let sit at room temperature for 30 minutes, turning and rearranging steaks for thorough marinating. Remove steaks from marinade and drain. (Retain used marinade for pit basting.) Place steaks on double-strength aluminum foil, turn up edges, and seal corners to make 2 or 3 shallow foil pans.

PIT BASTING

When pit fire is ready, place steaks in foil pans on grill 4 to 6 inches above pit fire. Liberally brush-baste every 3 to 5 minutes for 25 minutes. (Adjust dampers half open and close pit cover after each basting.) Steaks are done when they readily flake when poked with a fork in thickest portion.

Makes 6 servings

Hickory Lemon-Onion Whole Smoked Fish

The amounts in this recipe depend on the size of the fish. For larger fish, use the larger amounts.

    1 whole striped bass or salmon (3 to 12 pounds) or 2
        smaller fish (up to 12 pounds together) heads
        removed, cleaned, and scaled
    1/2 to 3/4 cube butter or margarine, melted
    2 to 3 medium onions, thinly sliced
    1/2 or whole medium-size bell pepper, thinly sliced, slices
        halved
    2 to 3 lemons, thinly sliced
    2 bay leaves per pound of fish
    1/2 to 3/4 quart Hickory Lemon-Onion Fish Marinade
        (recipe follows)
    1/4 to 1/2 pound hickory wood chips, watersoaked

TO PREPARE HICKORY LEMON ONION FISH MARINADE

(This amount is for a 3- to 6-pound fish. Double exactly for 8 to 12 pounds of fish.)

    1/2 cup fresh lemon juice, seeded
    1/2 cup (4 ounces) pure hickory liquid smoke
    1/3 cup *each* white wine vinegar, dry white wine
    1 tablespoon liquid onion

¹/₃ teaspoon *each* garlic parsley salt, black pepper, thyme
¹/₂ cube butter or margarine
1¹/₂ cups water

Combine marinade ingredients with water in a 2-quart pot on medium heat. Stir thoroughly and bring to a boil. Boil gently for 3 minutes. Set aside and let cool.

Yields ¹/₂ quart

TO MARINATE WHOLE FISH

With a damp cloth thoroughly wipe cleaned and scaled fish, including inside cavity. Place fish in a rectangular tight-fitting pan. Or use a very sturdy plastic bag set in a sizable rimmed pan. Pour marinade over fish. Cover pan or twist-tie plastic bag, submerging fish in marinade. Refrigerate for 1 hour or overnight. If using rectangular pan turn fish 2 or 3 times in marinade. Or turn plastic bag occasionally for thorough marinating.

PIT FIRE

Place 50-odd charcoal briquets in a mound and light. Let burn until white-ash-hot. Bank about 25 hot coals on each side of fire grill. Spread water-soaked hickory wood chips evenly over banked white-ash-hot charcoal. Let chips burn into pit fire until flames are out.

PAN PREPARATION AND PIT BASTING

Form triple-strength aluminum foil pan or pans to fit size of whole fish; each pan should have a cornersealed 1-inch rim all around so baste-marinade will not leak. (Or use sizable 1-inch rimmed throwaway aluminum pan.) Pour ¹/₄ cup of melted butter or margarine in bottom of pan then add 3 to 6 slices each onion and lemon and 2 to 3 bay leaves.

Remove fish from marinade and drain. (Retain used marinade for pit basting.) Pour or brush remaining melted butter or margarine inside fish cavity. Stuff fish with bay leaves and remaining slices of bell pepper, onion and lemon. Place fish in pan. Put a wad of foil under tail to keep it from cooking too fast.

Place pan 4 to 6 inches above fire, centered over space between banked coals. Baste fish every 5 minutes, cooking 10 to 12 minutes per 1 inch of thickest portion of fish. For a 2-inch fish baste and cook about 20 to 25 minutes; for 3 inches, 30 to 35 minutes. Fish is basically done if it readily flakes when prodded with a fork in thickest part. Allow ¹/₃ to ¹/₂ pound of fish per serving.

BARBEQUED BURGERS, SAUSAGES, AND DOGS

Onion-Pepper-Cheddar Hickory Burgers

3 pounds lean ground beef
1/2 pound grated cheddar cheese, mild or sharp (or use 8
    slices of cheese desired)
3 tablespoons tomato-base chili sauce (optional)
1/2 teaspoon *each* garlic parsley salt, seasoning salt, onion
    powder, black pepper
2 tablespoon *each* pure hickory liquid smoke, red wine
    vinegar, Worcestershire sauce, seeded lemon juice
1 egg, well beaten
8 thin slices onion (or finely chop 1 cup green onions)
8 thin slices red or green bell pepper rings (or finely chop
    them)
8 hamburger buns, split (or use kaiser buns)
Table bottles of vinegar pepper sauce and blended liquid
    smoke
1/4 pound hickory wood chips, water soaked

Condiments: Onions, dill pickles, sliced cucumbers,
    sliced avocado, lettuce, and any spreads desired

To lean ground beef in sizable pot or bowl add chili sauce (if desired),
salts, onion powder, black pepper, liquid smoke, vinegar, Worcestershire
sauce, lemon juice, and egg. Mix thoroughly and shape sixteen 1/4 inch-thick
patties. Divide cheese in 8 portions and place 1 portion or piece in center
of 8 patties, leaving a small border of meat around the cheese. Place slice

of onion or spoonful of green onions and a slice or spoonful of cheese, again leaving a border of meat. Place a second patty on top of each of the 8 patties, and press edges to seal in center ingredients, molding 8 burgers.

PIT FIRE

Presoak hickory wood chips in 2 cups water for 20 minutes and drain. Spread soaked chips over a close bed of 40-odd white-ash-hot charcoal briquets. Let chips burn into fire until flames are out.

PIT BASTING

When pit fire is ready, place burgers on lightly greased grill (or use hinged wire grill) 4 to 6 inches above pit fire. For medium-rare meat, brown 3 to 5 minutes on each side, sprinkle-basting browned sides with vinegar pepper sauce and blended liquid smoke. Place buns face down around edge of grill and toast until light brown. For well done, cook burgers a few minutes longer or until done the way you like them. If using barbeque sauce, brush it on burgers during last minutes of cooking time. Serve with or without sauce and with various condiments.

Makes 8 hearty servings

Cheesy Chili Bean Burgers

3 pounds lean ground beef
½ teaspoon *each* cayenne (red) pepper, garlic parsley salt
1 envelope onion soup mix
2 tablespoons *each* hickory liquid smoke, Worcestershire sauce, soft butter or margarine
1 egg, beaten
1 16-ounce can red chili beans, drained (save juice)
1 cup finely chopped green onions (scallions)
⅓ pound any cheese, grated
Bean juice chili sauce (recipe follows)
6 Italian or French round bread rolls
¼ pound hickory wood chips, water-soaked

In a sizable bowl or pot combine ground meat, cayenne pepper, garlic parsley salt, onion soup mix, liquid smoke, Worcestershire sauce, butter or margarine, and egg. Mix thoroughly. Shape sixteen 1/4-inch-thick patties. Spread drained beans equally on 8 patties only, leaving border of meat around beans. On top of beans spread finely chopped green onions and grated cheese, again leaving a border of meat. Place a second pattie on top of each of the first patties and press edges together to seal in center ingredients. Mold into eight burgers.

TO PREPARE BEAN JUICE CHILI SAUCE

Drained chili bean juice (approximately 1 cup)
3 tablespoons pure hickory liquid smoke
1/2 teaspoon spicy brown prepared mustard
1 dripping tablespoon honey or 1 heaping tablespoon
    brown sugar
3 tablespoons red wine vinegar
8-ounce can (1 cup) V-8 or tomato juice
3 tablespoons Worcestershire sauce
2 tablespoons fresh lemon juice, seeded
1 tablespoon chili powder (hot if desired)

Combine ingredients in a 2-quart pot on high heat. Stir thoroughly and bring to a boil. Reduce heat to medium low and boil gently for 10 minutes. Remove from heat.

PIT FIRE

Presoak hickory wood chips in water for 20 minutes and drain. Spread soaked chips over a close bed of 40-odd white-ash-hot charcoal briquets. Let chips burn into pit fire until flames are out.

PIT BASTING PIT-QUE BURGERS

Place patties on lightly greased grill 4 to 6 inches above pit fire (or use hinged wire grill). Brown 3 to 5 minutes on each side for medium rare, brush-basting with Bean Juice Chili Sauce. Or cook a few minutes longer, brushing on more sauce, until done the way you like them. Place buns, face down around edge of grill for light brown toasting. Serve on buns with remaining sauce spooned over more chopped green onions if desired.

Makes 8 servings

 # Spicy Hot French Bread Burgers

6 French bread rolls (6 inches long or round, split)
3 pounds lean ground beef
1/2 cup *each* Spanish onion, hot jalapeño peppers, finely
    chopped.

½ teaspoon *each* seasoning salt, garlic parsley salt, black
pepper, ground red hot or mild chili pepper
1 tablespoon *each* spicy hot brown prepared mustard,
hickory liquid smoke, Worcestershire sauce
½ quart Hickory-Quick Garlic-Pepper Baste (recipe
follows)
¼ pound hickory wood chips, baste- soaked

Condiments: Lettuce, sliced tomatoes, pickles, sliced
Spanish onion, sliced hot peppers, mayonnaise or
thick salad dressing (Russian or Thousand Island).

TO PREPARE HICKORY-QUICK GARLIC-PEPPER BASTE
½ cup *each* red wine vinegar, Worcestershire sauce
¼ cup fresh lemon juice, seeded
⅓ cup (3 ounces) pure hickory liquid smoke
1 tablespoon *each* liquid garlic, hot pepper sauce
3 cups water

Combine baste ingredients and water in a 2-quart pot on high heat. Bring
to a boil. Remove from heat and let cool.
Yields approx. 1 quart

TO PREPARE BURGERS
Combine ground beef, onions, jalapeño peppers, salts, black pepper,
mustard, liquid smoke, and Worcestershire sauce and mix thoroughly.
Tightly shape 6 round or long 8-ounce burger patties, ¾ inch thick.

PIT FIRE
Presoak hickory wood chips in 1 cup of baste for 20 minutes and drain.
Spread soaked chips over a close bed of 30-odd white-ash-hot charcoal
briquets. Let chips burn into fire until flames are out. Adjust damper vents
fully open.

PIT BASTING
Place patties on lightly greased grill 4 to 6 inches above pit fire (or use
hedged hinged wire grill). Brown 3 to 5 minutes on each side, liberally basting, for rare, or cook until done the way you like burgers. (If desired, brush
barbeque sauce during last 2 minutes of cooking). Place French bread rolls,
face down, around outer edge of grill and toast to a light brown. Serve with
condiments.
Makes 6 servings

Hickory-Smoked Rice Burger Pies

1¾ pounds lean ground beef
1¾ pounds lean ground pork
2 cups cooked beef Rice-a-Roni (approximately)
¾ cup *each* chopped scallions, chopped mushrooms
3 tablespoons *each* pure hickory liquid smoke, soy sauce,
    red wine vinegar, melted margarine
½ teaspoon *each* onion parsley salt, black pepper,
    blended or Italian herbs
1 large egg, beaten
1 quart Hickory-Quick Baste (recipe follows)
¼ pound hickory wood chips (baste-soaked)

TO PREPARE HICKORY-QUICK BASTE
½ cup *each* cider or red wine vinegar, Worcestershire
    sauce
¼ cup fresh lemon juice, seeded
⅓ cup (3 ounces) pure hickory liquid smoke
1 tablespoon *each* liquid garlic, liquid onion juice
3 cups water

Combine baste ingredients and water in a 2-quart pot on high heat. Bring to a boil. Remove from heat and let cool.
Yields approximately 1 quart

TO PREPARE BURGER PIES
Prepare beef Rice-a-Roni according to box directions. Measure out 2 cups and mix in scallions and mushrooms. Set aside.

To ground beef and ground pork, add liquid smoke, soy sauce, vinegar, margarine, onion parsley salt, black pepper, herbs, and egg. Mix well. Divide meat into 12 equal portions.

Shape 12 patties about ¼ inch thick. On 6 patties spread 2 heaping tablespoons Rice-a-Roni in the center equally. Place second patties on top and seal in Rice-a-Roni, lightly molding into burger pies with hands. Using double-strength foil, form 6 foil pans, or use one large rectangular throwaway aluminum pan.

PIT FIRE
Presoak hickory wood chips in 1 cup baste for 10 minutes and drain. Spread soaked chips over a close bed of 40-odd white-ash-hot charcoal briquets. Let chips burn into fire until flames are out. Adjust damper vents fully open.

PIT BASTING

Place burger pies in pans 4 to 6 inches above pit fire. Baste burgers every 3 or 4 minutes for 15 minutes or until done the way you like them. Serve immediately with sauce desired.

Makes 6 servings

Pit-Grilled Smoked Link Sausages

12 smoke link sausages, pork or all beef
1 quart Hickory-Quick Baste (page 81)
12 French bread or Hoagie rolls, 6 inches long, sliced
1/4 pound hickory wood chips, baste-soaked

Condiments: sliced dill pickles, sliced tomatoes, sliced or
     chopped onions, lettuce , mayonnaise or salad
     dressing, spicy or mild prepared mustard, and/or
     barbeque sauce desired

TO MARINATE LINK SAUSAGES

Poke fork holes through skin of link sausages all over. Pour 1/2 quart (2 cups) *warm* Hickory-Quick Baste over sausages in a tight-fitting container. Marinate for 30 minutes or refrigerate overnight.

PIT FIRE

Presoak hickory wood chips in 1 cup of baste for 10 minutes and drain. Spread soaked chips over a close bed of 30-odd white-ash-hot charcoal briquets. Let chips burn into fire until flames are out.

PIT BASTING

When pit fire is ready, remove link sausages from baste and drain. (Retain used baste for pit-basting.) Place link sausages on lightly greased grill 4 to 6 inches above pit fire. Brush- or spray-baste frequently, turning several times, for 10 to 12 minutes. Place rolls, face down, around edge of grill and toast until light brown or soft warmed, 2 to 3 minutes. Serve straight from the grill, *hot*, with display of condiments desired.

Makes 12 servings

Basic Hickory-Quick Hot Dogs

2 to 3 pounds hot dogs, thick style (pork, beef, chicken or turkey franks)
16 to 24 hot dog buns, split
1 quart Hickory-Quick Baste (page 81)
1/4 pound hickory wood chips, baste-soaked

Condiments: 2 to 3 cups finely chopped onions, thinly slice pickles or relish, 2 to 3 medium tomatoes (sliced and slices halved), lettuce if desired, warmed barbeque sauce if desired, spicy or mild prepared mustard, mayonnaise or salad dressing

TO MARINATE HOT DOGS
Poke fork hole through skin all over each frank. In a tight-fitting container pour 2 cups of warm baste over hot dogs. Marinate 30 minutes or refrigerate overnight.

PIT FIRE
Presoak hickory wood chips in 2 cups baste for 20 minutes and drain. Spread soaked chips over 30-odd white-ash-hot charcoal briquets. Let chips burn into fire until flames are out.

PIT BASTING
Remove franks from marinade and drain. (Retain used marinade for pit-basting.) Place hot dogs on lightly greased grill 4 to 6 inches above pit fire. Spray-baste and turn frequently for 3 to 5 minutes. (Brush on barbeque sauce if desired.) Place buns, split side down, around edge of grill until lightly toasted or softly warm. Serve immediately with condiments desired.
Makes 8 to 12 servings

Bobby-Qued Italian Sausage or Kielbasa

3 to 6 pounds Italian sausage (or Kielbasa) cut into 6- or 8-inch links
1 1/2 quarts Hickory-Quick Barbeque Baste-Marinade (page 20)
1 quart Hickory-Quick Barbeque Sauce (page 24)
1/2 pound hickory wood chips, baste-soaked

TO MARINATE SAUSAGE

Place cut sausages in a sizable bowl or pan. Pour enough baste over sausages to submerge them (approximately 2 cups). Marinate for 30 minutes to 1 hour at room temperature or refrigerate, covered, overnight.

PIT FIRE

Presoak the hickory wood chips in 1 cup of Hickory-Quick Barbeque Baste-Marinade for 20 minutes and drain. Spread soaked chips over a close bed of 40-odd white-ash-hot charcoal briquets. Let wood chips burn into fire until flames are out. When cooking sausages adjust damper vents three-fourths closed.

PIT BASTING

When pit fire is ready, remove sausages from marinade and place on lightly greased grill 4 to 6 inches above white-ash-hot pit fire (or place sausages in thin throwaway aluminum pan). Spray-baste or tong-dip in baste, turning every 3 to 5 minutes for 20 minutes. Tong-dip sausages in barbeque sauce during last 5 minutes of cooking time. Keep pit cover down after each spray-basting and saucing. When sausage are done the way you like them, serve hot off the grill with remaining barbeque sauce.

Makes 2 servings per pound

HICKORY-SMOTHERED AND STEW DISHES

 ## Bobby's Hickory Sirloin Chili

2 quarts Hickory-Quick Onion-Celery Barbeque Baste
  (recipe follows)
1 pound dried pinto beans, soaked in baste
2 cups chopped onions
2 cups chopped bell pepper (or use 1 cup bell peppers
  and 1 cup Jalapeño hot peppers)
1 cup finely grated carrots
3½ pounds sirloin steak (2 to 3 round sirloin steaks, cut
  ½ to ¾ inch thick).
½ cube margarine
½ cup (4 ounces) hot or mild red chili powder (or season
  to taste)
1 tablespoon *each* celery salt, parsley flakes, garlic
  parsley salt, ground black pepper
1 26-ounce can stewed tomatoes, chopped or use 4 to 5
  medium-size tomatoes, chopped
1 16-ounce can creamed corn

TO PREPARE BOBBY'S HICKORY-QUICK
ONION-CELERY BARBEQUE BASTE
1 cup red wine vinegar
½ cup fresh lemon juice, seeded
½ cup (4 ounces) pure hickory liquid smoke
½ cup *each* chopped onions, chopped celery

½ cup Worcestershire sauce (or substitute ⅓ cup
   Teriyaki sauce)
1½ quarts water

Combine ingredients with water in a 2-quart pot on high heat. Stir and bring to a boil. Reduce heat to medium and stew, covered, for 10 minutes. Remove from heat, let cool, and strain off 1 quart of liquid for pit-basting sirloin steaks. Use second quart, complete with stewed ingredients, to soak pinto beans.

Yields 2 quarts

TO PREPARE BEANS

Rinse pinto beans 3 times in clear water, removing all grit. In an 8-quart pot soak beans in second quart of baste-marinade for at least 1 hour. With pot on high heat, add 3 quarts water, 1 cup chopped onions, 1 cup bell peppersand (or substitute 1 cup Jalapeños), and grated carrots. Stew on medium heat for 2 hours, covered, or until beans are tender. Add 1, 2, or 3 cups water as necessary.

TO PREPARE MEAT — QUICK PIT- SMOKE AND PAN FINISHING

While beans are cooking sprinkle a handful of hickory wood chips into pit fire. Place whole steaks 4 to 6 inches above a close bed of 30-odd white-ash-hot charcoal briquets. Spray-baste steaks liberally, turning every 3 minutes and basting continuously for 20 minutes. After each turning and basting, close pit cover.

Remove steaks from pit grill. With a sharp knife on a cutting board cut steaks into ½ inch to ¾ inch cubes. Melt margarine in a 2-quart frying pan and add meat to pan. Over medium-high heat add remaining onions and bell peppers, chili powder, celery salt, parsley flakes, garlic parsley salt, and black pepper, stirring well into the meat. Cover and simmer-fry for 7 to 10 minutes. Add fried chili meat to pot of beans already cooked for 1 hour.

Add tomatoes. Thoroughly stir and bring to a boil. Reduce heat to medium, stirring every 10 minutes or so for 40 minutes. Add creamed corn. Cover and stir periodically for another 20 minutes or until beans are tender. Remove from heat and serve immediately.

Yields approximately 20 hearty servings

Note: Leftover chili can be refrigerated for 1 to 3 days, or frozen. This further enhances the seasoned hickory chili flavor. And as Andy Griffith might say, "Good! Gooood Chili! I mean, I tell *you*, you got something *good* heah!"

Hickory Smothered Pork Steaks

8 to 10 medium pork steaks (approximately 6 to 8 pounds)
1 teaspoon *each* garlic parsley salt, ground cloves, black
    pepper, dry mustard (from shakers)
2 cups pure vegetable oil

Pot Smother Ingredients

3/4 cup *each* finely chopped onions, celery, bell peppers
1 16-oz. can stewed tomatoes, chopped medium
3 ounces (1/3 cup) pure hickory liquid smoke
1/4 cup cider vinegar or red wine vinegar
1/4 cup fresh lemon juice, seeded
3 tablespoons brown sugar
1 tablespoon prepared mustard or spicy mustard
2 cubes or 1 tablespoon beef bouillon
1 quart water

Combine pot smother ingredients with water in a 6-quart pot on low heat. Stir thoroughly. From shakers, sprinkle coats of garlic parsley salt, ground cloves, black pepper, and dry mustard on both sides of meat. With fingers and hands press seasoning into pork steaks. If not using pit grill to brown steaks, lightly flour both sides, also pressing flour coating into meat.

PIT GRILL METHOD

Evenly spread a handful of hickory wood chips over 2 mounds of 30-odd white-ash-briquets. Place seasoned (unfloured) steaks on pit grill 4 to 6 inches above pit fire. Sear in coated seasonings, 2 to 5 minutes on each side, and remove from pit heat when each steak is browned. Note: When placing (unfloured) barbequed pork steaks in pot smother ingredients, add 2 tablespoons of flour thoroughly mixed with 1 cup of water to pot.

FRYING PAN METHOD

Heat 2 cups of vegetable oil in a 2-quart frying pan on medium-high heat. When oil is hot, add seasoned (floured) pork steaks to pan and fry until brown, about 2 to 5 minutes on each side. Drain frying oil from steaks and place them into pot smother ingredients.

FINAL SMOTHER-COOKING

Cover pot and smother-cook pork steaks on medium heat, stirring periodically, for 35 minutes or until tender. Saucy hickory-flavored barbeque gravy brews with smothering. Serve hot with any desired accompaniments.
Makes 6 to 8 servings

Pit-Range Hickory Beef Stew

2 to 2½ pounds lean beef stew meat cut into 1- to 2-inch
   pieces
1 teaspoon (approximately) *each* garlic parsley salt,
   seasoning salt, onion powder, black pepper (from
   shakers)
2 quarts Stew-Base Meat Marinade (recipe follows)
¼ pound hickory wood chips, soaked in stew base

Added Stew Ingredients
2 cups *each* carrots and celery, sliced ¼ inch thick
1 pound or 3 medium-size tomatoes (washed, wedge-cut
   in eights and cut again into bite-size pieces) or 1
   16-ounce can stewed tomatoes
⅓ pound string beans (washed, strings removed, and cut)
⅓ pound fresh English peas
4 or 5 medium-size russet or Idaho potatoes (thoroughly
   washed, peeled or unpeeled, and cut in bit-size pieces)
2 ears of corn (shucked, desilked, and kernels cut from
   cob)
10 or 12 small stewing onions, peeled for cooking
NOTE: For the beans, peas, and corn you can substitute a 10- to 20-ounce
frozen package of mixed vegetables.

TO PREPARE STEW-BASE MEAT MARINADE
¼ cup (2 ounces) pure hickory liquid smoke
½ cup Worcestershire sauce
¼ cup red wine vinegar
¼ cup fresh lemon juice, seeded
1 cup *each* finely chopped onions and bell peppers
1 tablespoon blended herb seasoning
5 cups water

Combine stew-base ingredients and water in an 8-quart pot on high heat.
Bring to a boil. Reduce heat to medium and stew for 10 minutes.

PIT FIRE
Presoak hickory wood chips in 1 cup of strained stew-base marinade for
20 minutes and drain. Spread soaked chips over a close bed of 30-odd white-
ash-hot charcoal briquets. Let burn into fire until flames are out.

SEAR SEASONING STEW MEAT

From shakers, sprinkle light coats of garlic parsley salt, seasoning salt, onion powder, and black pepper on both sides of stew meat. With fingers and hands press coated seasoning into meat. When pit fire is ready, place stew meat on lightly greased grill. Sear, brown, and seal in coated seasoning. Cook another 5 to 10 minutes on each side, liberally spray-basting as meat browns. Remove from pit.

ON THE RANGE

Place sear-browned stew meat in pot with stew-base marinade ingredients on high heat, stir and bring to a boil. Add carrots, celery, tomatoes, onions, and string beans. Stew, covered, for 30 minutes or medium-high heat. Add English peas, potatoes, and corn. (Any frozen vegetables should be added at the last 15 minutes of cooking time.) Stir and bring to a boil on high heat. Reduce heat to medium and stew for another 25 minutes, periodically stirring. Remove from heat. Serve hot.

Makes 8 to 10 servings

BARBEQUE SIDE DISHES

 ## Marshmallow-Orange Pit-Baked Sweet Potatoes

    6 medium-size sweet potatoes
    Orange Marshmallow Topping (recipe follows)
    4 strips crisply fried bacon, crumbled
To Prepare Orange Marshmallow Topping
    1 cube warm butter or margarine, melted
    1 cup orange juice
    1/4 *each* teaspoon cinnamon and nutmeg
    3 cups dice-size marshmallows (pressed in cup)
    3/4 cup skim milk

Combine topping ingredients with warm melted butter or margarine in a 2-quart pot over medium-low heat. Stir thoroughly and simmer for 5 to 7 minutes or until creamy smooth.

NOTE: Prepare this topping when sweet potatoes are already done. Serve it hot over baked sweet potato meat.

TO PIT-BAKE SWEET POTATOES

Wash sweet potatoes thoroughly. Rub very light coats of vegetable oil over each potato. Wrap in aluminum foil and place on pit grill 4 to 6 inches above a *loose* bed of 30-odd white-ash-hot charcoal. Bake with cover down for 50 minutes turning every 10 to 15 minutes, or bake until tender when pierced with a fork. Cut top open and fork up potato meat. Spoon on hot Orange Marshmallow Topping and garnish with crumbled bacon bits. Serve immediately.

Makes 6 servings

Hickory-Qued Baked Beans

    1 32- or 40-ounce can baked beans or 1 pound cooked
        navy beans
    6 slices lean bacon (beef if desired), cut crosswise into
        1/2-inch strips
    2 cloves minced garlic
    1 cup finely chopped onions
    ½ cup finely chopped red bell peppers
    1 cup ketchup (use hot-tasting ketchup if desired)
    1½ cups packed dark brown sugar
    or use 1 cup raw honey or molasses
    2 tablespoons dry mustard or 1 tablespoon regular or
        spicy prepared mustard
    2 tablespoons pure hickory liquid smoke
    3 or 4 strips crisply fried thick-sliced bacon for garnish

Preheat oven to 350 degrees. In a sizable frying pan, fry bacon until crispy but not burned. Add the garlic, onions, and bell peppers, and saute until onions are transparent. Combine sauteed vegetables and fat, all other ingredients and beans in a sizable mixing bowl or pot. Mix well. Pour beans into a 2- to 3-quart baking pan. Bake in oven uncovered for 45 minutes, or place on pit grill over 300-degree hickory chip charcoal fire for 1 hour with pit cover down. Garnish with crisp-fried bacon.
Makes 6 to 8 servings

Hickory-Hocked Black-Eyed Peas

    2 medium-size cured ham hocks
    ¼ cup vinegar
    ½ cup pure hickory liquid smoke
    1-pound package dried blackeyed peas
    3 cups finely chopped onions
    1 cup finely chopped bell peppers
    1 tablespoon *each* celery salt, garlic parsley salt,
        crumbled or ground bay leaf, ground black pepper.

TO PREPARE HICKORY HAM HOCKS

In a 6-quart pot on high heat parboil ham hocks for 1 hour, covered, in 4 quarts of water. Drain off water. To ham hocks add hickory liquid smoke, vinegar, and 3 quarts of fresh water. Boil on medium heat for another hour, covered.

TO PREPARE BLACK-EYED PEAS

While ham hocks are boiling, thoroughly wash black-eyed peas and soak in 3 quarts of water for 2 hours. Drain and add to pot with the boiled ham hocks, along with another quart of fresh water. Turn heat to high. Add onions, bell peppers, celery salt, garlic parsley salt, bay leaf, and black pepper, or season to taste desired. Thoroughly stir and bring to a boil. Reduce heat to medium. Let boil for 1½ hours or until peas are tender. Add ½ to 1 quart of water as needed during cooking time. Serve with rice (recipe follows).

TO PREPARE RICE

1½ cups long grain rice
1 teaspoon onion powder
¼ cube butter or margarine
3½ cups water

Wash rice once in cool water and drain. In a 3-quart pot combine onion powder and butter or margarine with water on high heat. Bring to a boil and immediately turn heat to extreme low. Immediately add rice, cover, and simmer for 22 minutes. Remove from heat and serve hot with Hickory-Hocked Black-Eyed Peas.

Makes 8 hearty servings

Hickory Honey-Seasoned Collard Greens

2 large or 4 small ham hocks
3 to 4 pounds garden fresh collard greens
½ cup pure hickory liquid smoke (1/4 cup for ham hocks,
    ¼ cup for greens)
3 medium-size onions (approximately 4 cups), chopped
1 cup *each* chopped bell peppers, chopped green onions
½ cup fresh hot peppers, chopped
1 tablespoon *each* garlic parsley salt, celery salt, black
    pepper

3 or 4 bay leaves

½ cup red wine vinegar

½ cup honey or ½ cup packed brown sugar

Condiments: Small bowls of finely chopped onions, finely chopped scallions, finely chopped hot peppers, table bottle of vinegar pepper sauce.

Thoroughly wash ham hocks and place them in 3 quarts water in an 8-quart pot on high heat. Add ¼ cup hickory liquid smoke, stir, and boil on high heat for 1 hour, covered. Remove from heat and drain.

Rinse greens and remove stems. Roll together several leaves at a time and cut across leaves to make 1 inch strips. Put cut greens in pot with par-boiled ham hocks. Add 2 quarts water, onions, bell peppers, green onions, hot peppers, salts, black pepper, and bay leaves. Turn heat to high. Stir in remaining hickory liquid smoke, vinegar and honey. Cover, bring to a boil covered. Reduce heat to medium. Periodically stir and let cook for approximately 2 hours or until very limp or done as desired. Serve hot with condiments and corn bread (pages 99 and 101).

Makes 6 to 10 hearty servings

 # Pinto Beans 'n' Rice

THE BEANS

1 pound dried pinto beans or red beans

½ to 1 pound thick-sliced cured pork (beef or pork bacon)

1 cup onions, finely chopped

1 cup bell peppers, very finely chopped

3 tablespoon *each* cider vinegar, pure hickory liquid smoke

1 teaspoon *each* garlic parsley salt, hot or mild chili powder

1 teaspoon *each* black pepper, paprika, seasoning salt, onion powder, celery salt (or substitute 1 envelope — 1¼ ounce — onion soup mix)

4 quarts water

In clear water rinse pinto beans 3 times in a 6-quart pot. Fill pot with 4 quarts fresh water. Let beans soak 2 hours. Add all remaining ingredients and put on high heat. Reduce heat to medium. Boil covered for 2 hours. (If you didn't have time to soak the beans, boil them for 3½ hours.) Add water as needed every ½ hour or so, cooking until beans are tender and bean broth is "bean" tasty. Serve hot over butter-steamed long grain rice in bowl.

THE RICE
1½ cups long grain rice
⅓ cube butter or margarine
½ teaspoon salt
3½ cups water

Combine butter or margarine and salt with water in a 2-quart pot on high heat. Bring to a quick boil and reduce heat to very low. Pour rice evenly into steaming hot water. Cover and cook for 22 minutes or until rice is grain-for-grain fluffy and still firm. Serve hot with pinto beans in bean broth juices.
Makes 6 to 8 servings

Baked Bacon-Cheddar Macaroni Cheese

1-pound box small elbow macaroni
1 cube butter or margarine
¾ pound mild, medium or sharp cheddar cheese
    (crumble half and slice half 1/16-inch thick)
5 or 6 strips bacon, crisply fried and crumbled (reserve
    bacon grease to saute vegetables)
¾ cup *each* finely chopped green onions, chopped celery,
    finely chopped red bell peppers
1 cup milk
½ teaspoon (approximately) *each* seasoning salt, onion
    parsley salt, black pepper, onion powder, celery salt,
    garlic powder from shakers

Combine ¼ cube of butter or margarine and macaroni in 4 quarts boiling water in a 6-quart pot. Stir, reduce heat to medium, and cook for 10 minutes. Remove from heat and drain off water. Into hot macaroni thoroughly stir ¾ cube of butter or margarine and crumbled cheddar cheese.

Saute green onions, celery, and bell peppers for 3 minutes on medium-low heat. Do not brown. Combine macaroni, crumbled bacon, sauteed vegetables, and milk, mixing thoroughly. From shakers or with measuring spoon season mixture with ½ teaspoon each of seasoning salt, celery salt, onion parsley salt, black pepper, onion powder, and garlic powder (or season to taste). Mix thoroughly.

Preheat oven to 300 degrees. Into a 4-quart baking dish or pan pour half of macaroni mixture and spread flat. Place half the sliced cheese on this first layer. Pour remaining macaroni mixture into pan and spread flat. Place rest of sliced cheese on top of this last layer. Bake for 15 minutes covered with aluminum foil and for 5 minutes more uncovered or until top of baked macaroni cheese is golden brown.

Makes 6 to 8 hearty servings

Southern Creole String Beans

2 pounds fresh green beans (washed, strings removed, and cut into 1 to 1 1/2-inch pieces)
3 to 4 medium-size russet or Idaho potatoes, 2 to 3 pounds (washed, peeled, and cut in 1-inch bite-size cubes)
1 cup finely chopped onions
2 or 3 bay leaves
1/2 pound thick-sliced hickory-cured bacon (slices cut in thirds and limp-fried or 1/2 pound cured ham ends quick fried for 2 minutes in 1/4 cube margarine)
1/2 cup *each* finely chopped red bell peppers, finely chopped scallions (green onions)
1/2 teaspoon gumbo filé
1 teaspoon *each* ground black pepper, garlic parsley salt, celery salt, dry parsley
2 tablespoons *each* cider vinegar, hickory liquid smoke
2 quarts water

Combine green beans, onions, scallions, bell peppers, bay leaves, liquid smoke and vinegar with water in a 6-quart pot on high heat. Bring to a boil, reduce heat to medium, and cover. Limp-fry bacon or ham ends for 1 to 2 minutes and add to pot, along with bacon grease or margarine. Add gumbo file, black pepper, garlic parsley salt, and celery salt. Boil gently on medium heat for 30 minutes. Add potatoes on top of green beans in pot, sprinkle dry parsley on potatoes, and cook another 20 minutes. When potatoes are done (easily poked with a fork), stir beans lightly. Serve hot, using a slotted spoon to include a little liquid with each serving. Accompany with cornbread (pages 99 – 100).

Makes 8 hearty servings

Corn, Gumbo (Okra), and Tomatoes

A delectably perfected country southern recipe which I got from my mother. Originally consisting of corn, okra, and tomatoes only, the contemporary seasoning touch is my own.

$1/2$ cube margarine (substitute butter if desired)
$1/2$ to $3/4$ pounds fresh okra, washed and cut in 1/4- to
    1/2-inch pieces
$1/2$ cup *each* finely chopped bell pepper, finely chopped
    scallions (green onions)
1 pound (3 medium-size) fresh tomatoes, cut in eight
    wedges and wedges cut in half
3 ears of corn (de-silked and kernels cut from cob) or
    10-ounce package of frozen corn
1 cup sliced mushrooms
$1/2$ teaspoon *each* onion parsley salt, black pepper, gumbo
    filé, celery salt
20 medium-size fresh shrimp (optional)

In wok or 3-quart frying pan melt margarine and stir-fry okra, bell peppers, and scallions, slightly browning for 3 to 4 minutes on medium heat. Add tomatoes, corn, and mushrooms. Add remaining seasonings, stir thoroughly, and cover. Simmer for 5 to 7 minutes. (Add shrimp if desired and cook for 3 to 5 more minutes.) Remove from heat and serve hot with Bacon-Cheddar Southern Corn Bread (page 99).

Makes 6 servings as side dish; with shrimp added, makes 4 a la carte servings

Pit-Qued Corn on the Cob

6 ears of corn, shucked and de-silked
$1/2$ cube melted butter or margarine

2 tablespoons pure hickory liquid smoke
2 tablespoons honey
1 tablespoon vinegar
1 cup water

Place ears of corn on individual sheets of double-strength aluminum foil. Each sheet should be long and wide enough for wrapping each ear. Melt butter or margarine on medium-low heat. Add water and stir in liquid smoke, honey, and vinegar. Simmer about 3 minutes. Remove from heat. Pour 2 or 3 tablespoons of mixture over each ear of corn set in aluminum foil. Wrap loosely, folding sides and twisting ends shut. Place on pit grill 4 to 6 inches above 30-odd white-ash-hot coals for 15 to 20 minutes, turning every 5 minutes.

Makes 6 servings

Honey-Seasoned Mustard and Turnip Greens

³/₄ pounds sliced cured pork or beef (or use smoked
     turkey parts)
2 pounds fresh leafy mustard greens
2 pounds fresh young turnip greens with turnip roots
1 cup *each*, chopped onion, chopped red or green bell
     peppers, chopped scallions
2 or 3 bay leaves
1 teaspoon *each* black pepper, garlic parsley salt, onion
     powder, celery salt
¹/₂ cup red wine vinegar or cider vinegar
¹/₄ cup (2 ounces) pure hickory liquid smoke
2 quarts water

Condiments: Small bowls of chopped onions and finely
     chopped hot peppers; table bottle of vinegar pepper
     sauce

Parboil cured pork or beef for 30 minutes in 2 quarts of water on medium-high heat, covered. Drain off water and rinse twice. Wash mustard and turnip greens, pick stems off, and cut 1-inch strips across leaves. Wash turnip roots, cut off stem tops and bottom root strings, and cut roots into bite-size pieces. Combine all ingredients in 2 quarts water in 6-quart pot on high heat and bring to a boil. Reduce heat to medium and cook, covered,

for 30 minutes for vitamin retention or 60 minutes for southern-style tenderness. Serve immediately with condiments and corn bread.
Makes 6 to 8 hearty servings

Bacon-Cheddar Southern Corn Bread

1 cup yellow cornmeal
1 cup all-purpose flour (or sifted whole wheat flour)
2 tablespoons baking powder
1 tablespoon onion salt
1½ cups milk
½ cup melted butter or margarine (substitute bacon
   grease for southern taste)
½ cup minced green onions
2 large or 3 small eggs
3 tablespoons vegetable oil
6 strips crisply fried bacon, crumbled
¾ cup mild, medium, or sharp cheddar cheese, grated

Combine cornmeal, flour, baking powder, and onion salt in a sizable mixing bowl and blend thoroughly with a spoon. Add milk, melted butter or margarine (or bacon grease), green onions, and eggs. Stir and spoon-beat for 2 minutes until smooth, or beat in mixer for 1 minute. Warm vegetable oil on medium-low heat in a cast-iron frying pan or rectangular baking pan. Pour half of batter into pan. Evenly sprinkle in crumbled bacon bits and cheddar cheese. Pour in remaining batter. Bake in preheated 350-degree oven for 25 minutes, or bake in pit 4 to 6 inches above a banked bed of hot charcoal (with pit thermometer registering 375 degrees) for 30 minutes, pit cover down and damper vents adjusted fully open, until bread is brown and top springs back when touched.
Makes 8 to 10 servings

Hickory Chili-Seasoned French Bread

1 cube (1/4 pound) butter or margarine at room
   temperature

¼ cup minced scallions (young green onions)
1 tablespoon hickory liquid smoke (optional)
1 tablespoon liquid garlic
2 tablespoons mild or hot chili powder
1 loaf French bread (16- to 20-ounce size), cut lengthwise

Combine melted butter and minced scallions in a 1-quart pan over low heat. Stir in liquid smoke, liquid garlic, and chili powder, mixing thoroughly, and remove from heat. Spoon or brush chili-garlic-butter mixture on bread halves so butter soaks down into bread. Place bread on aluminum foil, cut side up, then onto pit grill 4 to 6 inches above a loose bed of 30-odd *hot*, half-burnt coals for 5 minutes. Cut loaf halves across in slanted 1- or 2-inches wide pieces.

Makes 8 to 12 piece servings

Southern-Style Corn Bread Muffins

8 strips bacon
1 cup yellow cornmeal
1 cup all-purpose flour
1 tablespoon baking powder
1 teaspoon onion salt
2 dripping tablespoons honey (or substitute ½ cup sugar)
2 extra-large eggs or 3 small or medium eggs
1½ cups buttermilk or substitute regular milk
1 cup of grated cheddar cheese or 1 cup pimento, onion,
    or chive cream cheese (optional)

Place bacon strips in a sizable frying pan on medium heat and cook to a crispy brown. (Retain ½ cup of bacon grease.) Crumble bacon strips. In a mixing bowl thoroughly blend cornmeal, flour, baking powder, and onion salt. (Blend in sugar if *not* using honey.) Add eggs and bacon grease and buttermilk. Beat vigorously 2 minutes (or 1 minute in electric mixer) and stir in crumbled bacon bits. Add batter to dry ingredients and mix thoroughly. (Add honey at this point if not using sugar.) Mix until everything is smoothly combined.

Preheat oven to 375 degrees. In a 1/2-cup muffin pan, thoroughly grease each muffin cup with ½ teaspoon vegetable oil. If making bacon-cheese combination, use about two-thirds of batter to fill each muffin cup half full and spoon approximately ¾ teaspoon of cheddar cheese or cream cheese in each cup. Pour in remaining batter. Bake for 20 minutes.

Makes 6 to 12 servings

SALADS

Uncle Tom's Texas Green Salad

The very last time I visited my Uncle Tom in 1951 I watched him make up his own personal salad several times. The ingredients varied sometimes depending on what was leftover. Later in life I came up with my own salads, remembering Uncle Tom's — particularly several of his uncommon salad ingredients. While this chef-style salad recipe may at first seem common, some of my Uncle Tom's *uncommon* ingredients — drained leftover black-eyed peas, bits of leftover barbeque meat, corn bread "kruttons" (croutons), along with his blue and cottage cheese dressing — will tickle your taste buds.

1 clove garlic, cut in half lengthwise
4 to 6 cabbage leaves (use greener outside leaves)
1 cup watercress leaves, stems trimmed
Several romaine lettuce leaves, in bite-size pieces
Several spinach leaves, in bite-size pieces
1 5- to 6-inch cucumber, unpeeled and slices 1/8 inch thick
1 cup diced, sliced or coarsely grated carrots
2 celery stalks, thinly sliced
1/2 cup peppers, finely chopped
2 medium tomatoes, each cut into 8 to 12 wedges and
     then halved
10 to 20 raw onion rings (use purple salad onion if
     desired)
4 hard-boiled eggs, quartered
1/2 cup pimento olives
1 cup leftover chopped barbequed pork, chicken, or beef

1 cup leftover black-eyed peas or 1 cup canned
    black-eyed peas, drained
2 cups crumbled corn bread for "kruttons"
$\frac{1}{2}$ cup cottage cheese
$\frac{1}{2}$ cup blue cheese, finely crumbled
$\frac{1}{2}$ cup pure vegetable oil
4 tablespoons red wine vinegar
1 tablespoon salad herbs (mixture of thyme, tarragon,
    oregano, sweet basil)
$\frac{1}{4}$ teaspoon *each* garlic parsley salt, onion salt, ground
    black pepper (or to taste)

Thoroughly rub salad bowl with cut garlic; throw garlic away. Add and toss in bowl all bite-size pieces of cabbage, lettuce, and spinach. Add grated carrots, eggs, olives, barbeque meat, black-eyed peas, and corn bread "kruttons." To prepare salad dressing, blend cottage cheese, blue cheese, oil, and vinegar together and pour dressing over salad ingredients. Lightly toss and season with salad herbs, parsley salts, and pepper. Or use any staple salad seasoning desired and season to taste. Serve right away.
Serves 6 to 10

 # Goober* Carrot Raisin Slaw

4 medium-size carrots, washed and finely grated
1 cup cabbage (white or red), finely grated
$1\frac{1}{3}$ cup raisins
1 cup crushed black walnuts
1 cup mayonnaise or salad dressing
$\frac{1}{2}$ teaspoon *each* ground black pepper, onion parsley salt
    (or to taste)
Parsley for garnish

In a 3- or 4- quart bowl combine and mix together grated carrots, cabbage, 1 cup raisins, and walnuts with mayonnaise or salad dressing. Season to taste with black pepper and onion parsley salt. Garnish with bits of fresh parsley and remaining $\frac{1}{3}$ cup of raisins.
Makes 6 to 8 servings

---

*Generic African meaning for "nuts," not peanuts.

Cottage Cheese Goober* Fruit Salad

Actually I originally got this quick salad recipe from my father. But the tasty orange peel and bacon bit garnish is my own. A fruit cottage cheese salad that's almost a savory dessert to top off a hearty barbeque meal.

    1 16-ounce can fruit cocktail, juice drained
    1 pound cottage cheese
    2 cups chopped pecans or black walnuts
    1 teaspoon dry ground orange peel
    Iceberg lettuce leaves for serving
    3 strips crisply fried bacon, crumbled for garnish

Combine ingredients in sizable mixing bowl and mix loosely. Spoon on to loose lettuce leaves on individual plates and garnish each salad dish with a teaspoon of crumbled bacon bits.
Makes 6 servings

Hunky Crunchy Potato Salad

My mother used to make some very tasty potato salad. But it was more or less a tasty quasi-mashed potato salad which came from overcooking the potatoes and overmixing. Some years ago my wife Leslie and I hunk-cut the potatoes and eggs — and added various crunchy ingredients.

    6 medium to large baking potatoes (Idaho or russet),
        unpeeled
    8 large hard-boiled eggs (6 cut in quartered hunks, 2
        sliced for garnish)
    1 cup chopped purple salad onions
    1 cup chopped celery
    ½ cup finely chopped scallions (green onions)
    1 cup diced dill pickle
    1 cup finely chopped red and/or green bell peppers

Generic African meaning for "nuts," not peanuts.

½ teaspoon *each* paprika, seasoning salt, garlic parsley
   salt, onion salt, ground black pepper (from shakers),
   or season to taste
½ cup dill pickle juice
1½ to 2 cups mayonnaise or salad dressing

Garnish: 2 sliced hard-boiled eggs, sprinkled paprika and
   parsley.

In a 6-quart pot, cook potatoes on medium-high heat, covered, for 20 minutes or until they are fork tender. (Cook only 15 minutes if potatoes are small.) Drain and let sit in cold water. Boil eggs for 12 to 15 minutes maximum. Also drain and let sit in cold water. Peel potatoes, cut them in 3/4-inch hunks, and place in a mixing bowl.

To the potatoes add the 6 hunk-cut eggs, onions, celery, scallions, pickles, and bell peppers. With a large spoon tumble the ingredients, periodically sprinkling and mixing in the paprika, salts, and black pepper. Add dill pickle juice and mayonnaise. Transfer the mixed salad to your best-looking bowl and garnish with sliced boiled egg, more sprinkled paprika, and small pieces of fresh parsley around the edges. Refrigerate covered, or keep cool in cooler if at an outdoor barbeque.

Makes 8 to 10 hearty servings

 # Hunky Crunchy Macaroni Salad

¼ cube margarine
1-pound package large or small elbow macaroni
8 large hard-boiled eggs, cut in 8 hunks
1 cup chopped onions (use mild red Bermuda, if desired)
1 cup celery, chopped or 1/8-inch slant-sliced
1 cup diced dill pickles
½ cup grated carrots
½ cup chopped pimento olives
1 cup red and/or green bell peppers, finely chopped
1 tablespoon blended salad herbs
1½ to 2 cups mayonnaise
½ teaspoon *each* seasoning salt, garlic parsley salt,
   coarse ground black pepper, paprika (from shakers),
   or season to taste

Garnish: Fresh parsley, paprika, pimento, olives

Put 3 quarts of water in a 6-quart pot, add margarine, stir slightly, and add macaroni. Boil on medium-high heat for 15 minutes and drain. Let cool a bit. Combine and thoroughly mix eggs, vegetables, and herbs. Add mayonnaise and shaker seasonings. Garnish.

Makes 8 to 10 hearty servings

Beet Spinach Special

1 tablespoon liquid garlic
2 bunches or ¾ pound fresh crispy spinach, torn into
    bite-size pieces
⅓ pound (2 pressed cups) bean sprouts
⅔ of 16-ounce can sliced beets, pickled if desired and cut
    in halves
1 or 2 cups any seasoned croutons (optional)

Dressing Ingredients
1/4 cup pimentos, finely chopped
2 hard-boiled eggs, finely chopped
2 tablespoons mayonnaise
1 cup pure vegetable oil
4 tablespoons red wine vinegar
2 tablespoons blended Italian herbs
¼ teaspoon *each* celery salt, lemon pepper seasoning (or
    season to taste)

With cloth or paper towel rub salad bowl with liquid garlic. Loosely toss spinach and bean sprouts in salad bowl. Add beets and loosely toss (add croutons if desired). Place all dressing ingredients in mixing bowl or blender, except celery salt and lemon pepper seasoning, and slowly blend for ½ minute. Pour dressing over salad, toss, and season to taste with celery salt and lemon pepper seasoning. Serve right away.

Makes 4 to 6 servings

SALT FREE, LOW SODIUM, AND SUGARLESS BARBEQUE DISHES AND ACCOMPANIMENTS

Hickory-Qued Beef Spareribs
(Salt Free)

3 to 5 pounds beef spare ribs (slabs cut in 2- or 3-rib pieces)
1 quart Salt-Free Hickory-Herbal Tomato Baste-Marinade (recipe follows)
1/2 teaspoon *each* paprika, black pepper, onion powder (from shakers)
Hickory-Herbal Barbeque Sauce (page 131)
1/4 pound hickory wood chips, water-soaked

TO PREPARE SALT-FREE HICKORY-HERBAL TOMATO MARINADE
Vegetables

3/4 cup Spanish onions, chopped
3/4 cup scallions (green onions), chopped
1/2 cup red or green bell peppers, chopped
1 cup celery, chopped
1 clove garlic, chopped
3 medium-size tomatoes, finely chopped or pureed

Staples

 3 bay leaves
 1 tablespoon oregano
 1 teaspoon dry mustard (spicy hot if desired)
 $\frac{1}{2}$ teaspoon ground pepper
 $\frac{1}{2}$ teaspoon rosemary leaves

Liquid Seasonings

 $\frac{1}{2}$ cup (4 ounces) pure hickory liquid smoke
 $\frac{1}{2}$ cup dry red sherry
 $\frac{1}{2}$ cup red wine vinegar
 $\frac{1}{2}$ cup fresh lime juice, seeded
 $\frac{1}{2}$ cup fresh lemon juice, seeded
 1 quart water

Combine vegetables and staples in water in a 4-quart pot on high heat. Bring to a boil. Reduce heat to medium and stew for 30 minutes, covered. Set aside and let cool. Strain off stewed ingredients and stir in liquid seasonings. Bring to a quick boil. Reduce heat to medium low and simmer for 5 minutes. Remove from heat.

Yields 1 quart plus

TO MARINATE BEEF RIBS

Place rib pieces in a close-fitting container or a sturdy plastic bag set in a rimmed pan. Pour half baste-marinade to submerge ribs. Cover container or twist-tie plastic bag. Marinate 1 to 2 hours at room temperature or refrigerate overnight. Turn occasionally for thorough marinating.

PIT FIRE

Presoak hickory wood chips in 2 cups of water for 20 minutes and drain. Spread soaked chips over 40-odd white-ash-hot charcoal briquets. Let wood chips burn into pit fire until flames are out.

SEAR SEASONING

When pit fire is ready, remove rib pieces from marinade and drain. (Retain used marinade for pit basting.) From shakers, sprinkle very light coats of black pepper, onion powder, and paprika on both sides of ribs, using fingers and hands to press and rub in seasonings all over, including edges. Place rib pieces on lightly greased grill 4 to 6 inches above pit fire. Sear, brown, and seal in coated seasoning, 3 to 5 minutes on each side.

PIT BASTING

Liberally brush-baste browned rib pieces, then turn and baste again every 10 minutes (pit cover down after each basting) for $1\frac{1}{2}$ to 2 hours or until done the way you like beef ribs. Brush on saltless, sugarless barbeque sauce every 5 to 10 minutes during last 30 minutes of cooking time.

Makes 4 to 6 servings

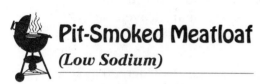

Pit-Smoked Meatloaf
(Low Sodium)

2½ to 3 pounds lean ground beef
1 quart Quick Pit-Baste (recipe follows)
Hickory-Herbal Barbeque Sauce (page 131)
¼ pound hickory wood chips, baste-soaked

Meat Seasonings
½ cup margarine for sauteing vegetables
¼ cup onions, finely chopped
¼ cup red or green bell peppers, finely chopped
⅓ cup celery, finely chopped
½ cup carrots, finely chopped or grated
2 medium-size tomatoes, very finely chopped
2 tablespoons hickory liquid smoke
½ teaspoon *each* Italian herbs, rosemary leaves
1 teaspoon dry mustard
1 large egg, well beaten

TO PREPARE QUICK PIT-BASTE
½ cup (4 ounces) hickory liquid smoke
¼ cup red wine vinegar
½ cup cooking sherry (salt free)
½ cup fresh lemon juice, seeded
3 cups water

Combine baste ingredients in water in a 4-quart pot on high heat. Bring to a boil. Turn heat down to medium low and simmer for 7 minutes. Remove from heat.

Yields approximately 1 quart

PIT FIRE
Presoak hickory wood chips in 1 cup of Quick Pit-Baste. Spread soaked chips over a white-ash-hot bed of 40-odd charcoal briquets. Adjust damper vents half open.

SAUTEING VEGETABLES

In a 2-quart frying pan melt margarine and add onions, bell peppers, celery, and carrots. Saute on medium-low heat for 3 minutes or until onions are transparent. Do not brown. Add 1/2 cup of water and stir in tomatoes. Add liquid smoke and sprinkle in Italian herbs, rosemary leaves, and dry mustard, stirring thoroughly and cooking for another 3 minutes.

MIXING AND SHAPING MEAT LOAF

In a sizable bowl combine lean ground beef with sauteed ingredient and mix thoroughly. Mix in well-beaten egg with hands. Place meat loaf on double-strength aluminum foil or use 1-inch-rimmed throwaway aluminum pan. Shape meat into round or square loaf 2 1/2 to 3 inches thick.

PIT BASTING

Place meat loaf in pan on pit grill 4 to 6 inches above pit fire. Let cook and become firm for 15 to 20 minutes with pit cover down. Then spray- or brush-baste every 15 minutes for 1 1/2 hours or until meat loaf is done. Serve immediately with saltless, sugarless Hickory Herbal Barbeque Sauce.

Makes 6 to 8 servings

Spicy Hickory-Qued Short Ribs
(Salt Free)

3 pounds lean beef short ribs, cracked and marinated
1 quart Hickory Pepper Baste-Marinade (recipe follows)
1/2 teaspoon *each* onion powder, ground red chili
    powder, ground black pepper, garlic powder (from
    shakers)
2 cups Hickory-Herbal Barbeque Sauce (page 131)
1/4 pound hickory wood chips, baste-soaked

TO PREPARE HICKORY PEPPER BASTE-MARINADE
Vegetables

3/4 cup chopped Spanish onions
1/2 cup chopped hot jalapeño peppers (fresh produce)
1/2 cup chopped red bell peppers
3/4 cup chopped scallions (green onions)
1 cup chopped celery

Staples

1 teaspoon pure ground hot red chili powder
1/4 teaspoon ground cumin

½ teaspoon spicy hot dry mustard
2 cubes beef bouillon extract

Liquids

½ cup (4 ounces) hickory liquid smoke
¾ cup red wine vinegar
¾ cups fresh lime juice, seeded
1 quart water

Combine vegetables and staples on water in a 4-quart pot on high heat. Bring to a boil. Reduce heat to medium and stew for 30 minutes, covered. Set aside and let cool. Strain off stewed ingredients. Add and stir in all liquid ingredients. Bring to a quick boil and reduce heat to medium low. Simmer covered for 7 minutes.

Yields 2 quarts plus

TO MARINATE SHORT RIBS

Place short ribs in a tight-fitting pot or bowl or use a plastic bag set in a rimmed pan. Pour in enough baste-marinade to cover short ribs (approximately 2 cups). Cover or twist-tie plastic bag. Marinate 2 hours at room temperature or refrigerate overnight. Turn occasionally for thorough marinating.

PIT FIRE

Presoak hickory wood chips in 1 cup of baste-marinade for 20 minutes and drain. Spread half of soaked hickory chips over 40-odd white-ash-hot charcoal briquets. Allow chips to burn into pit fire until flames are out. Add second half of baste-soaked chips halfway through cooking time. Adjust damper vents approximately half open.

SEAR SEASONING

When hickory charcoal pit fire is ready, remove short ribs from marinade and drain. (Retain and strain used marinade for pit basting.) From shakers sprinkle light coats of onion powder, ground red chili powder, black pepper, and garlic powder on all sides and edges of each short rib. Use fingers and hands to press and rub in coated seasonings. Place rib pieces on pit grill 4 to 6 inches above hot pit fire. Sear, brown, and seal in seasonings for 2 minutes on each of four rib sides, with pit cover down.

PIT BASTING

Spray- or brush-baste short ribs before and after each turning, every 10 minutes (pit cover down after each basting) for 50 minutes or until done the way you like short ribs. Brush on Hickory-Herbal Barbeque Sauce or fork- or tong-dip each short rib in sauce every 5 minutes during last 15 minutes of cooking time.

Makes 6 servings

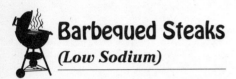

Barbequed Steaks
(Low Sodium)

4 *each* T-bone or porterhouse steaks, cut ¾ to 1 inch thick
¾ quart Hickory Margarine Baste-Marinade (recipe
    follows)
2 cups Hickory-Herbal Barbeque Sauce (page 131)
¼ pound hickory wood chips, baste-soaked

TO PREPARE HICKORY MARGARINE BASTE-MARINADE
Vegetables
½ cup each onions, scallions, bell pepper, celery, chopped

Staples
½ teaspoon *each* onion powder, celery powder, ground or
    crumbled bay leaves, black pepper, ground oregano,
    paprika

Liquids
¼ cup (2 ounces) pure hickory liquid smoke
½ cup dry red wine
¼ cup red wine vinegar
⅓ cup fresh lemon juice, seeded
½ cube unsalted margarine (substitute unsalted butter if
    desired)
¾ quarts water

Combine vegetables and staples in water in a 2-quart pot on high heat. Bring to a boil. Reduce heat to medium low and stew for 30 minutes. Remove from heat and let cool slightly. Strain off stewed ingredients from liquid. Hold unsalted margarine and add all other liquid ingredients. Stir, bring to a boil, and remove from heat. Separate out 1 cup for baste-soaking hickory wood chips. Add unsalted margarine to rest of hot marinade and stir until combined.

TO MARINATE STEAKS
Slash fat edges of steaks once or twice to keep from curling on pit grill. Place steaks in a flat, tight-fitting pan. Pour approximately half of hot baste-marinade into pan. Cover all surfaces, pouring marinade in between steaks and also setting steaks on top of one another to allow marinade to reach

bottom of pan. Marinate at room temperature for 1 hour or refrigerate over-night, covered. Turn steaks occasionally for thorough marinating.

PIT FIRE

Presoak hickory wood chips in reserved baste for 20 minutes and drain. Spread soaked hickory chips over a close bed of 40-odd white-ash-hot char-coal briquets. Let wood chips burn into pit fire until flames are out.

PIT BASTING

Remove steaks from marinade and drain briefly. (Retain used marinade for pit basting if needed.) Place steaks on pit grill 4 to 6 inches above hot pit fire. For rare steaks turn once, spray- or brush-basting with margarine baste-marinade, browning each side for 3 to 5 minutes. For medium or well-done steaks turn and baste again, pit cover down, and keep basting until done the way you like them. Serve with sauce.

Makes 4 servings

Herbed Hickory-Qued Rib Steaks
(Low Sodium)

4 rib steaks, cut ½ to ¾ inch thick
1 quart No Salt Quick Baste-Marinade
1 tablespoon blended Italian herbs (from shaker)
2 tablespoons onion powder (from shaker)
Hickory-Herbal Barbeque Sauce (page 131, optional)
¼ pound hickory wood chips, water soaked

TO PREPARE NO SALT QUICK BASTE-MARINADE

¼ cup (2 ounces) pure hickory liquid smoke
½ cup cider vinegar
½ cup fresh lemon juice, seeded
3 cups water

Combine all ingredients in a 2-quart pot on high heat. Stir and bring to a boil. Remove from heat and let cool.

Yields 1 quart

TO MARINATE RIB STEAKS

In a tight-fitting container pour approximately half of baste-marinade over steaks. Marinate for 1 hour at room temperature or refrigerate over-night.

PIT FIRE

Presoak hickory wood chips in 1 cup of baste-marinade for 20 minutes and drain. Spread soaked wood chips over a close bed of 40 white-ash-hot charcoal briquets. Let chips burn into fire until flames are out.

PIT-QUE BASTING

Remove rib steaks from marinade and drain thoroughly. (Retain used marinade for pit basting.) Sprinkle coats of onion powder and blended Italian herb seasoning on both sides of steaks. Rub and press coated seasoning into meat. Place on pit grill 4 to 6 inches above hot charcoal briquets. Brown steaks 2 minutes on each side. Basting browned sides, turn and baste twice and cook 3 to 5 minutes on each side for rare meat, or baste and cook a few more minutes until done the way you like rib steaks. Serve with Hickory-Herbal Barbeque Sauce if desired.

Makes 4 servings

Hickory Burger Special
(Low Sodium)

1¼ pound extra lean ground beef (sirloin)
⅓ teaspoon *each* onion powder, garlic powder, black
    pepper, crushed red pepper, celery powder or celery
    seeds
4 slices any low-salt cheese
4 thin slices bell pepper rings
2 cups Margarine Hickory Baste (recipe follows)
8 slices no- or low-sodium rye bread
¼ pound hickory wood chips, baste-soaked

Condiments: Crispy leaf spinach, thin slices of tomato,
    thin slices of onion, thin slices of cucumber, sliced
    hard-boiled egg, any no- or low salt thick salad
    dressing

TO PREPARE MARGARINE HICKORY BASTE

3 tablespoons pure hickory liquid smoke
3 tablespoons red wine vinegar
3 tablespoons fresh lemon juice, seeded
1 teaspoon blended Italian herbs
¼ cube unsalted margarine
2 cups water

Set margarine aside. In a 2-quart pot combine all other baste ingredients with water on high heat. Bring to a boil, then simmer for 2 minutes on low heat. Remove from heat. Separate out 1 cup for baste-soaking hickory wood chips. To remaining baste add margarine, and stir until melted.

TO PREPARE GROUND SIRLOIN

Combine onion powder, garlic powder, lemon pepper seasoning, crushed red pepper, celery powder, and beef, thoroughly. Shape 8 very flat wide patties. Place a folded slice of cheese and a slice of bell pepper on 4 patties, leaving a border of meat all around. Place second patty on top of first and seal edges, molding with hand 4 burger specials.

PIT FIRE

Presoak hickory wood chips in reserved baste for 10 minutes and drain. Spread soaked chips over close bed of 20-odd white-ash-hot charcoal briquets. Let chips burn into fire until flames are out.

PIT BASTING

Place burgers on lightly greased grill 4 to 6 inches above pit fire. As burgers brown, spray- or brush-baste and cook 2 to 3 minutes on each side for medium rare, or cook until done the way you like them. Lightly toast rye bread slices on grill if desired. Serve sandwiches immediately with thick salad dressing and other condiments desired.

Makes 4 servings

Texas-Qued Pork Spareribs
(Salt Free)

2 slabs pork spareribs (approximately 6 pounds)
2 quarts Uncle Tom's No salt Sugarless Barbeque
    Baste-Marinade (recipe follows)
1/2 teaspoon *each* black pepper, garlic powder, onion
    powder, parsley flakes, paprika (from shakers)
2 cups Hickory-Herbal Barbeque Sauce (page 131)
1/2 pound hickory wood chips, baste-soaked

TO PREPARE UNCLE TOM'S NO SALT SUGARLESS BARBEQUE BASTE-MARINADE
Vegetables

2 cups *each* onions, red or green bell peppers, scallions,
    celery, chopped
1 garlic clove, minced

Rinds of 4 lemons, cut up (hold juice for liquid
   ingredients).

Staples
   1 teaspoon *each* black pepper, onion powder, garlic
      powder
   1 tablespoon parsley flakes
   2 bay leaves

Liquids
   1 cup (8 ounces) pure hickory liquid smoke
   1 cup red wine vinegar
   3/4 cup fresh lemon juice, seeded (from 4 lemons)
   1 1/2 quarts water

In a 6-quart pot, combine vegetable and staple ingredients with 1 1/2
quarts water over high heat. Bring to a boil. Turn heat down to medium and
stew, covered, for 30 minutes. Remove from heat and let cool. Strain off all
stewed ingredients and stir in all liquid ingredients. Bring to a quick boil.
Reduce heat to medium low and simmer for 5 minutes. Remove from heat
and let cool. (Using hot marinade – 150 degrees – is also good, but do not
use a plastic bag.)
   Yields approximately 2 quarts

TO MARINATE SPARERIBS
   Place rib slabs in a rectangular pan, or cut slabs in half and place in plastic bag set in a rimmed pan. Pour in approximately 1 quart marinade to submerge ribs. Cover pan or twist-tie plastic bag. Marinate for 2 hours at room
temperature or refrigerate overnight. Turn occasionally for thorough marinating.

PIT FIRE
   Presoak hickory wood chops in 2 cups of baste-marinade for 30 minutes
and drain. Spread half of soaked hickory chips over close bed of 40-odd
white-ash-hot charcoal briquets. Let chips burn into fire until flames are
out.

SEAR SEASONING
   When pit fire is ready, remove ribs from marinade and drain. (Retain and
strain used marinade for pit spray-basting.) From shaker, sprinkle light
coats of black pepper, garlic powder, onion powder, parsley flakes, and paprika on both sides of ribs. With hands and fingers press and rub in coated
seasoning. Place ribs on pit grill 4 to 6 inches above hot pit fire. Sear, brown,
and seal in seasonings for 3 to 5 minutes on each side.

PIT BASTING

Spray- or brush-baste browned ribs, turn and baste again. Repeat every 10 to 15 minutes (closing pit cover after each basting) for 3 hours. Add second half of presoaked hickory chips after first hour of cooking. Keep basting liberally for total cooking time or until done the way you like ribs. Brush on Hickory-Herbal Barbeque Sauce every 5 minutes during last 20 minutes of cooking time.

Makes 4 servings

Saucy-Qued Country-Style Ribs
(Salt Free)

3 pounds country-style ribs
1 teaspoon (approximately) *each* black pepper, onion powder, parsley flakes, blended seasoning (no salt, sugar, or MSG), celery seed, cayenne red pepper (from shaker)
1½ quarts No salt Quick Baste-Marinade (recipe follows)
1 quart Hickory-Herbal Barbeque Sauce (page 131)
½ pound hickory wood chips, baste-soaked

TO PREPARE NO SALT QUICK BASTE-MARINADE
1 cup cider or red wine vinegar
1 cup fresh lemon juice, seeded
½ cup (4 ounces) pure hickory liquid smoke
2 tablespoons liquid garlic or 1 garlic clove, minced
4 tablespoons liquid onion or 1 cup finely chopped onions
2 bay leaves
1 quart water

Combine all ingredients in a 3-quart pot on high heat. Bring to a boil. Reduce heat to medium and simmer 5 minutes. Remove from heat and let cool.

Yields 1½ quarts

TO MARINATE RIBS
Place ribs in a tight-fitting container or in a sturdy plastic bag set in a rimmed pan. Pour half of baste-marinade over ribs. Cover container or twist-tie plastic bag. Marinate for 4 hours at room temperature or refrigerate overnight. Turn occasionally for thorough marinating.

Presoak hickory wood chips in 2 cups baste-marinade for 30 minutes and drain. Spread soaked chips over a close bed of 40 to 50 white-ash-hot charcoal briquets. Let chips burn into fire until flames are out.

SEAR SEASONING

When pit-fire is ready, remove ribs from marinade and drain. (Retain and strain used marinade for pit spray-basting.) From shakers, sprinkle medium coats of blended seasoning, onion powder, celery seed, parsley flakes, black pepper, and cayenne pepper on both sides of ribs. With fingers and hands press seasonings into meat. Place ribs on lightly greased grill 4 to 6 minutes above hot pit fire. Sear and brown for 3 to 5 minutes on each side, sealing in coated seasonings.

PIT BASTING

Turn and spray- or brush-baste browned ribs every 10 minutes for 60 minutes or until done the way you like them. Tong-dip ribs in Hickory-Herbal Barbeque Sauce every 5 minutes during last 30 minutes of cooking time. Serve with remaining heated sauce.

Makes 4 to 6 servings

Pit-Qued Pork Loin Chops
(Salt Free)

These loin chops can be pit-qued *or* browned under the broiler and cooked in the oven.

 4 center-cut loin pork chops (1 inch thick)
 1 quart No salt Lemon-Orange Baste-Marinade (recipe follows)
 1/2 teaspoon *each* black pepper, ground cloves, garlic powder, onion parsley powder (from shakers)
 2 1/2 quarts Hickory-Herbal Barbeque Sauce (page 131)
 1/4 pound hickory wood chips, baste-soaked

TO PREPARE NO SALT LEMON-ORANGE BASTE-MARINADE
Vegetables
 1/2 cup *each* scallions, bell peppers, celery, chopped

Liquids
 3/4 cup fresh lemon juice, seeded
 1 cup fresh orange juice
 1/2 cup cider vinegar

³/₄ cup (6 ounces) pure hickory liquid smoke
3 cups water

In a 3-quart pot combine vegetable and liquid ingredients with water on high heat. Bring to a boil. Turn heat down to medium low. Stew for 25 minutes, covered. Remove from heat, let cool, and strain off all stewed vegetables to leave baste liquid.

Yields approximately 1 quart

TO MARINATE CHOPS

Place chops in a container or plastic bag. Pour half of baste-marinade to submerge over chops. Cover container or twist-tie bag. Marinate 1 to 2 hours at room temperature or refrigerate overnight.

PIT FIRE

Presoak hickory wood chips in 1 cup of baste-marinade. Spread soaked chips over a close bed of 20-odd white-ash-hot charcoal briquets. Let chips burn into fire until flames are out.

SEASONING CHOPS

When pit fire is ready, remove chops from marinade and drain. (Retain used marinade for pit basting.) Sprinkle light coats of black pepper, ground cloves, garlic powder and onion parsley powder on both sides of chops. Use fingers and hands to press seasoning into chops.

PIT BASTING METHOD

Place chops on pit grill 4 to 6 inches above pit fire. Brown chops 3 to 5 minutes on each side. Brush-baste browned sides, turning and basting every 10 minutes for 40 minutes until meat near bone is no longer pink or until done the way you like chops. Serve immediately with Hickory-Herbal Barbeque Sauce.

BROILER-OVEN METHOD

Place seasoned chops in pan under 450-degree broiler, browning chops for 2 to 3 minutes on each side. Remove from broiler and place in oven. Reduce oven heat to 375 degrees. Pour 1 cup of baste-marinade over chops. Bake covered, spoon-basting every 15 minutes and adding more baste-marinade as needed. During last 15 minutes of cooking time pour 1 cup of Hickory-Herbal Barbeque Sauce over chops. Total cooking time is 40 minutes or until chops are done the way you like them.

Makes 4 servings

Glazed Hickory-Smoked Pork Steaks
(Salt Free)

4 pounds lean pork steaks (approximately 8 steaks)
3 cups Hickory Pineapple Lime-Mint Baste-Marinade
    (recipe follows)
1½ quarts Hickory-Herbal Barbeque Sauce (page 131)
1 cup hickory wood chips, water-soaked

TO PREPARE HICKORY-PINEAPPLE LIME-MINT BASTE-MARINADE

½ cup unsweetened pineapple juice
½ cup fresh orange juice, seeded
½ cup fresh lime or lemon juice, seeded
½ cup pure hickory liquid smoke
½ cup red wine vinegar
1 garlic clove, minced
6 to 8 whole cloves
¼ teaspoon ground black pepper
½ teaspoon *each* dry mustard, crumbled dry mint (or
    several fresh mint leaves)
2 cups water

Combine all ingredients in a 3-quart pot on high heat. Stir and bring to a boil. Continue to boil for 5 minutes. Remove from heat.
Yields 1 quart plus

TO MARINATE STEAKS

Place pork steaks in a tight-fitting container and cover with hot marinade. Marinate at room temperature for 1 hour.

PIT FIRE

Presoak hickory wood chips in 1 cup of water for 30 minutes and drain. Spread soaked chips over a solid bed of 30-odd white-ash-hot charcoal briquets. Let chips burn into fire until flames are out.

PIT BASTING

When pit fire is ready, remove steaks from marinade and drain. (Retain used marinade for pit basting.) Brown steaks 3 to 5 minutes on each side. Brush-baste, turn, and brush-baste other side every 10 minutes (closing pit cover after each basting) for 40 minutes or until done the way you like them. Serve immediately with Hickory-Herbal Barbeque Sauce.
Makes 4 to 6 servings

Pineapple Lime-Mint Pit-Qued Lamb Chops
(Low Sodium)

8 lamb chops, cut ¾ to 1 inch thick
Dry mint seasoning, black pepper (from shakers)
1 quart Hickory Pineapple Lime-Mint Baste-Marinade
    (page 122)
1 quart Apple-Lime-Mint Barbeque Sauce (page 25)
½ pound hickory wood chips, baste-soaked

TO MARINATE LAMB CHOPS

Place chops in a close-fitting container or in a sturdy plastic bag set in a rimmed pan. Pour 2 cups of warmed marinade over chops if using metal pan or 2 cups of cool marinade if using plastic bag. Marinate chops at room temperature for 1 hour or refrigerate overnight.

PIT FIRE

Presoak hickory wood chips in 1 cup of baste-marinade for 20 minutes and drain. Spread soaked chips over a close bed of 30-odd white-ash-hot charcoal briquets. Let chips burn into fire until flames are out. Adjust damper vents half open.

SEAR SEASONING AND PIT BASTING

When pit fire is ready, remove lamb chops form marinade and drain. (Strain through a fine sieve and retain used marinade for pit spray-basting.) Sprinkle light coats of dry mint seasoning and black pepper on both sides of chops. With hands press and rub seasonings into meat. Place chops 4 to 6 inches above hot pit fire. Sear and brown meat for 2 to 3 minutes on each side, sealing in seasonings. Brush- or spray-baste after browning, turning and basting every 7 minutes for 20 minutes for medium rare or until done the way you like lamb chops. (Close pit cover after each basting.) Brush on Apple-Lime-Mint Barbeque Sauce 2 or 3 times during last 5 or 10 minutes of cooking time. Serve immediately.

Makes 4 hearty servings.

Pit-Qued Roaster Chicken
(Low Sodium)

5- to 7-pound roaster chicken

1½ quarts No salt Hickory Buttered Baste-Marinade
   (recipe follows)
½ quart Hickory-Quick Barbeque Sauce (page 24)
½ pound hickory wood chips, baste-soaked

TO PREPARE NO SALT HICKORY BUTTERED BASTE-MARINADE

Vegetables

1 cup *each* chopped onions, bell peppers, celery,
   scallions, grated carrots
2 cloves garlic, finely chopped
Rinds of 4 medium-size lemons, cut up (hold for liquid
   ingredients)

Staples

1 tablespoon blended seasoning (no salt, sugar, or MSG)
2 bay leaves
½ teaspoon *each* thyme, sage, oregano, basil

Liquids

¾ cup (6 ounces) pure hickory liquid smoke
1 cup red wine vinegar
¾ cup fresh lemon juice, seeded (from 4 medium-size
   lemons)
1 teaspoon liquid hot pepper seasoning (optional)
¾ cube unsalted butter or unsalted margarine
1¼ quart water

Set butter aside. In a 4-quart pot combine vegetable, staple, and liquid ingredients with water on high heat. Bring to a boil. Reduce heat to medium. Stew, covered, for 25 minutes. Remove from heat and strain off vegetables from liquid. (Separate out 1½ cups for baste-soaking of hickory wood chips.) Add butter to remaining warm baste and stir until melted.
   Yields approximately 1½ quarts

TO MARINATE ROASTER CHICKEN

Place chicken in a tight-fitting container or in a sturdy plastic bag set in a rimmed container. Pour half of buttered baste-marinade over roaster chicken, submerging it, or twist-tie plastic bag, for thorough marinating. Marinate at room temperature for 2 hours or refrigerate overnight.

PIT FIRE

Presoak hickory wood chips in reserved baste-marinade. Spread soaked chips over a close bed of 40 to 50 white-ash-hot charcoal briquets. Let burn into pitfire until flames are out. Adjust damper vents half open.

PIT BASTING

Remove roaster chicken from marinade and slightly drain. (Retain and strain used marinade for spray-basting.) Set roaster in aluminum pan and place on pit grill 4 to 6 inches above fire. Liberally spray- or brush-baste roaster every 15 minutes for 2 hours (pit cover closed after each basting) or, if using meat thermometer, until it shows done. If desired, brush on barbeque sauce during the last 30 minutes of cooking time.

5-pound roaster makes 6 to 8 servings

Hickory-Smoked Turkey Breast
(Low Sodium)

6-to 10-pound turkey breast or 4- to 6-pound breast half
2 quarts Hickory Butter-Herb Baste-Marinade (recipe
    follows)
1/2 pound hickory wood chips, baste-soaked

TO PREPARE BUTTERY BASTE-MARINADE FOR TURKEY
Vegetables
1 cup *each* onions, bell peppers, carrots, celery, scallions,
    chopped
2 cloves garlic, finely chopped

Staples
2 bay leaves
1 tablespoon *each* parsley flakes, concentrated chicken
    bouillon (Low sodium), poultry seasoning
3 tablespoons blended seasoning (no salt, sugar, or MSG)
    including paprika, red pepper, black pepper, dry
    mustard, ginger, oregano, rosemary, celery seed,
    granulated garlic and onion

Liquids
1 cup pure hickory liquid smoke
1/2 cup red wine vinegar
3/4 cup fresh lemon juice, seeded
1 cube unsalted butter or unsalted margarine
2 quarts water

Combine vegetable and staple ingredients with water in a 4-quart pot on high heat. Bring to a boil. Reduce heat to medium and stew, covered for 35 minutes. Remove from heat. Strain off stewed ingredients from liquid.

Set butter aside. Add liquid smoke, vinegar, and lemon juice to liquid in pot. Simmer on medium-low heat for 10 minutes. Remove from heat. Separate out 2 cups for baste-soaking hickory wood chips. Add butter or margarine to remaining hot baste-marinade and stir until melted.

Yields 2 quarts plus

TO MARINATE TURKEY BREAST

Place turkey breast in a sizable tight-fitting container or in a sturdy plastic bag set in a rimmed pan. (Note: If using frozen turkey it must be completely thawed.) Pour approximately 1 quart of baste-marinade over turkey. Cover container or twist-tie plastic bag, submerging breast in marinade. Marinate 2 hours at room temperature or refrigerate overnight. Turn occasionally for thorough marinating.

PIT FIRE

Presoak hickory wood chips in reserved unbuttered baste-marinade for 20 minutes and drain. (Retain used baste for more soaked chips if needed.) Bank 50-odd white-ash-hot charcoal briquets (25 or so on each side) along two sides of pit grate. Place drip pan on coal grate in center of charcoal. Spread one-half of soaked chips evenly over banked hot charcoal. Add second half of soaked chips midway through total cooking time. Add charcoal briquets as needed. Adjust damper vents one-fourth open.

PIT BASTE

When pit fire is ready, remove turkey breast from marinade and slightly drain. If desired, debone for easy carving. (Retain used marinade for pit brush-basting.) If using a meat thermometer, insert it in thickest part of breast. Place breast on pit grill 4 to 6 inches above drip pan. Liberally brush-baste every 20 to 30 minutes (pit cover down after each basting and damper vents adjusted three-fourths closed). Cook for 2 to 3 hours or until golden brown. (Meat thermometer should register 185 degrees for done.) Remove turkey breast from pit and let sit for 10 minutes before carving. Serve hot or refrigerate covered, to serve cold.

Allow 2/3 pound (uncooked) per serving.

Saucy Hickory Pit-Qued Chicken
(Salt Free)

2 boiler-fryer chickens, quartered
1¼ quart Hickory-Herbal Barbeque Sauce (page 131)

$^{1}/_{2}$ cup *each* pure hickory liquid smoke, red wine vinegar,
fresh seeded lemon juice
2 cups lukewarm water
6 to 8 cups hickory wood chips, water soaked

TO MARINATE CHICKEN QUARTERS

Combine 2 cups Hickory-Herbal Barbeque Sauce, the liquid smoke, vinegar, and lemon juice in slightly heated water and stir thoroughly. Place chicken in sizable container and pour saucy marinade over it. Marinate for 3 hours at room temperature or refrigerate overnight. Turn occasionally for thorough marinating.

PIT FIRE

Presoak hickory wood chips in water for 20 minutes and drain. Spread half of soaked chips over a close bed of 50-odd white-ash-hot charcoal briquets. Let chips burn into pit fire until flames are out. Add second half of soaked chips midway through total cooking time. Adjust vents half open.

PIT BASTING

When pit fire is ready remove chicken from saucy marinade and drain slightly. (Retain used marinade for pit basting.) Turn and baste or tong-dip in marinade every 10 minutes (closing pit cover after each basting) for 60 minutes or until meat is no longer pink near bone. Brush on Hickory-Herbal Barbeque Sauce every 10 minutes during last 30 minutes of cooking. Serve with remaining heated sauce.

Makes 6 to 8 servings

Hickory Smothered Cacciatore Chicken
(Low Sodium)

$3^{1}/_{2}$- to 4-pound broiler-fryer, cut in 8 to 10 pieces
1 cup vegetable oil
$^{1}/_{2}$ cube margarine
No salt, sugarless blended seasoning (from shaker)
1 cup whole wheat flour
$^{1}/_{4}$ cup yellow or white cornmeal

SMOTHER INGREDIENTS

1 clove garlic, finely minced
$^{1}/_{2}$ cup *each* celery, bell peppers, chopped
1 cup *each* carrots, onions, chopped

$1/3$ cup *each* hickory liquid smoke, red wine vinegar, fresh
   seeded lemon juice, seeded
3 bay leaves
3 medium-size tomatoes, finely chopped
$1/2$ tablespoon *each* celery seed, onion parsley powder,
   paprika, thyme, sage, dry mustard
1 teaspoon liquid hot pepper sauce (optional)
4 cups water

Combine all smother ingredients with water in a 6-quart pot on medium-low heat. Cover and simmer while preparing chicken. On medium heat warm vegetable oil in a wide-base 3- or 4-quart frying pan or a wok. Melt margarine in heated vegetable oil just before adding chicken.

Sprinkle medium coats of blended seasoning on all sides of chicken pieces. With hands press seasoning into meat. Pour whole wheat flour and cornmeal into a plastic bag or sturdy paper bag and shake to blend. Place seasoned chicken pieces in meal-flour bag and shake for complete coating.

Place chicken pieces in hot oil/and margarine. Immediately reduce heat to medium low. Fry chicken a few minutes on each side to brown. Immediately place each browned half-cooked chicken piece in pot of heated smother ingredients. Let chicken smother on medium heat, covered for 30 to 40 minutes or until ready to fall off the bone. Serve hot.

Makes 5 to 6 servings

Saucy Vegetable and Fish Kabobs
(Low Sodium)

2 pounds halibut steaks cut in $1^1/4$ inch cubes (or use
   salmon or $1^1/2$ pounds scallops)
1 quart Lemon-Orange Fish Sauce (recipe follows)
1 pound fresh broccoli tops, cut (cook thick stems 5
   minutes to prepare them for skewering)
1 dozen tiny new potatoes (washed, unpeeled, and
   cooked 10 minutes)
1 basket cherry tomatoes
2 medium-size green bell peppers (seeded and cut in 1
   1/4-inch squares)
4 cups hickory wood chips, water soaked

TO PREPARE LEMON-ORANGE FISH SAUCE

Vegetables

3/4 cup *each* chopped onions, celery, bell peppers
   (blender pureed)
2 cloves minced garlic
1/4 cup minced parsley
3 or 4 minced mint leaves

Liquids

1/2 cup (4 ounces) pure hickory liquid smoke
1/2 cup *each* fresh lemon juice and fresh orange juice,
   seeded
1/2 cup red wine vinegar
1 6-ounce can tomato paste
1/4 cube margarine
2 cups water

Staples

1/2 teaspoon *each* black pepper, basil, oregano, dry
   mustard, ground cinnamon, ground ginger, chili
   powder, lemon pepper seasoning
1 tablespoon no salt, sugarless blended seasoning

In a blender puree vegetable ingredients with 1 cup of water. Rinse out blender with the second cup of water, combining pureed vegetables with liquid ingredients in a 4-quart pot on high heat. Add and stir in all staple ingredients, bringing to a boil. Reduce heat to medium and cook uncovered, stirring frequently, for 45 minutes or until sauce reduces to approximately 1 quart. Set aside and let cool. If prepared 1 to 2 days in advance, refrigerate. Let sauce come to room temperature just before using or reheat slightly.
   Yields 1 quart

PIT FIRE

Presoak hickory wood chips in water for 30 minutes and drain. Spread soaked chips over a close bed of 30-odd white-ash-hot charcoal briquets. Let chips burn into fire until flames are out.

TO MARINATE FISH CUBES

Wipe fish cubes with a damp cloth. In a sizable container combine room-temperature Lemon-Orange Fish Sauce with 1 cup water. Place fish cubes or scallops in sauce submerging each piece. Let sit for 30 minutes to 1 hour refrigerated. Lightly turn occasionally for thorough marinating. Lift each fish cube or scallop directly from marinade to skewer.

PIT BASTING

With vegetables washed, cut, and/or cooked, thread fish cubes on 4 to 6 sturdy skewers, alternating a different vegetable between each fish cube or scallop. (If desired, dip each vegetable in sauce as it is skewered. Do skewering process over long rectangular pan to catch any sauce that drips.) Heat sauce on pit grill. Place vegetable-fish kabobs on a well-greased grill 4 to 6 inches above pit fire. Brush-baste with sauce several times, turning occasionally and cooking for about 10 minutes or until fish readily flakes when forked. Serve with remaining heated sauce.

Makes 6 servings

Stir-Fried Shrimp Gumbo (Okra) Vegetables
(*Low Sodium*)

½ pound fresh okra washed, stems removed, and cut
    across in 1/4-inch pieces
½ cup chopped scallions
½ cup vegetable oil
½ cube margarine
3 medium-size tomatoes, chopped
2 ears of corn, 2 de-silked, washed, and kernels cut from
    cob
2 tablespoons *each* fresh seeded lemon juice, hickory
    liquid smoke, wine vinegar
½ teaspoon gumbo filé
1 tablespoon blended seasoning (no salt, sugar, or MSG)
3 medium-size raw shrimp, shelled and deveined
2 or 3 fresh mint leaves, minced
¼ cup fresh parsley

In a wok or wide-base frying pan, saute okra and scallions in heated margarine and vegetable oil for 3 to 5 minutes on medium heat, slightly browning. Add tomatoes, corn, mint, parsley, liquid smoke, lemon juice, vinegar, blended seasoning and gumbo Filé and stir thoroughly. Add shrimp, stir-frying for another 3 to 5 minutes. Remove from heat and let sit, covered for 2 minutes. Serve hot.

Makes 4 to 6 servings

Hickory-Herbal Barbeque Sauce
(Salt Free, Sugarless)

Vegetables and Fruit
$\frac{1}{2}$ cup *each* onions, scallions, bell peppers, carrots,
    celery, finely chopped
4 medium-size tomatoes, chopped
1 medium-size green cooking apple, chopped
1 *each* garlic clove, minced
$\frac{1}{2}$ cup hot green chili peppers, chopped (or less to taste)

Staples
1 tablespoon *each* onion powder, garlic powder, spicy dry
    mustard
1 tablespoon *each* black pepper, ground red chili pepper,
    celery flakes, parsley flakes, crumbled or powdered
    bay leaves, rosemary
1 teaspoon *each* ground clove, ground ginger, basil
2 tablespoons or 3 cubes beef bouillon

Liquids
1 cup (8 ounces) pure hickory liquid smoke
1 cup red wine vinegar
$\frac{1}{2}$ cup *each* lemon juice and lime juice, seeded
$\frac{1}{4}$ cup salt-free prepared mustard
$\frac{1}{2}$ cup dry cooking sherry cooking
3 cups water

Blender puree all vegetables and fruit together, rinsing blender contents with the 3 cups water into a 6-quart pot on high heat (include water). Add staple and liquid ingredients. Stir thoroughly and bring to a boil. Reduce heat to medium. Boil gently uncovered for 30 minutes, stirring every few minutes, and covered for another 30 minutes, stirring frequently, for a total cooking time of 1 hour. Sauce should have thickened a little by then; cook longer if needed. Remove sauce from heat until ready to use, or store in refrigerator.

Yields $1\frac{1}{2}$ to 2 quarts

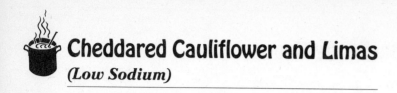

Cheddared Cauliflower and Limas
(Low Sodium)

⅓ pound cured (smoked) turkey parts, parboiled
1⅓ cups fresh shelled baby lima beans (approximately 1
    pound in pods) or 10-ounce package frozen baby lima
    beans
⅓ cup *each* finely chopped onions, bell peppers
½ cube unsalted margarine or unsalted butter
1 teaspoon vegetable seasoning or blended herb
    seasoning
½ teaspoon *each* black pepper, onion parsley powder,
    celery seed
1 tablespoon vinegar
⅔ pound (approximately 10 ounces) fresh cut cauliflower
    sprouts or 10-ounce package frozen cut cauliflower
¼ cup chopped pimentos
4 to 5 ounces low sodium or salt-free mild cheddar
    cheese, sliced ⅛ inch thick

In a 2-quart pot parboil turkey parts in 4 cups of water on high heat for 20 minutes, covered. Remove from heat. Drain and rinse twice with clear warm water to reduce salt and fat.

In a 2-quart wide-base pot or sauce pan combine fresh shelled lima beans, parboiled turkey parts, chopped onions and bell peppers, margarine, vegetable seasoning or herb seasoning, black pepper, onion parsley powder, celery seed, and vinegar in 4 cups of water on medium-high heat. Bring to a boil. Reduce heat to medium and cook for 30 minutes, covered. Add cauliflower, cover, and cook another 20 minutes. Stir in pimentos the last 2 minutes of cooking time. Total cooking time for fresh limas and cauliflower is 50 minutes. Turn off heat. Spread sliced cheddar cheese over hot limas and cauliflower in pot, covering it so cheese melts, and serve immediately. (Or serve hot on plate, placing a slice of cheese over each serving.)

Makes 6 servings

NOTE: If using frozen limas and cauliflower, cook limas 20 minutes and frozen cauliflower 15 minutes for a total cooking time of 35 minutes.

Hickory-Seasoned Collard Greens
(Low Sodium)

⅓ pound cured turkey parts
½ cup *each* chopped onions, scallions, bell peppers,
    celery
1 bay leaf
2 cloves finely chopped garlic
½ teaspoon *each* black pepper, red pepper, dry mustard,
    ground ginger, celery seed, rosemary, onion powder,
    oregano (or use 2 tablespoons blended seasoning
    with no salt, sugar, or MSG)
2 tablespoons pure hickory liquid smoke
3 tablespoons red wine vinegar
1½ pounds collard greens or kale, washed, picked, and
    cut 1 inch across leaf

Parboil turkey parts for 40 minutes in 2 quarts water on medium-high heat, covered. Drain and rinse twice. In a 4-quart pot combine parboiled meat, chopped onions, scallions, bell peppers, and celery in 1 quart water on medium-high heat. Stir in all other ingredients. Add cut greens and cover. Cook 35 minutes for vitamin retention or 60 minutes for southern-style tenderness. Serve with slotted spoon.
Makes 4 to 5 servings

Creole String Beans
(Low Sodium)

¼ pound cured beef or pork
¾ pound fresh green beans, washed, strings removed,
    and cut into 2-inch pieces
½ teaspoon gumbo filé
1 bay leaf
1 tablespoon vinegar
¾ cup finely chopped onions
⅓ cup finely chopped bell peppers
¾ pound russet or Idaho potatoes, washed, unpeeled,
    and cut into bite-size cubes

³⁄₄ teaspoon *each* coarse black pepper, ground red
    pepper, garlic powder, parsley flakes, celery seed,
    onion powder

Parboil cured beef or pork for 40 minutes and rinse twice to remove salt. Combine green beans, parboiled meat, parsley flakes, celery seed, onion powder, garlic powder, gumbo filé, bay leaf, vinegar, onions, and bell peppers in 1½ quarts water in a 4-quart pot on medium-high heat. Bring to a boil. Reduce heat to medium low. Boil gently for 30 minutes, covered. Add potatoes to top of beans in pot. Sprinkle in red pepper and coarse black pepper. Cover and cook for 20 minutes. Stir lightly when potatoes are easily poked with a fork. Serve from pot with ladle with holes in it.
Makes 4 servings

Peppered Spinach Greens
(Low Sodium)

1 pound leaf spinach, cut in bite-size pieces
1 medium red or green bell pepper, seeded and coarsely
    chopped
1 tablespoon salt-free, sugarless blended seasoning
½ teaspoon *each* vegetable seasoning, all-spice, cayenne
    red pepper, black pepper, vinegar, hickory liquid
    smoke
¼ cube margarine

Condiments: Table vinegar, pepper sauce

Garnish: Chopped green onions, sliced hard-boiled egg

Combine ingredients except condiments and garnish in 2 cups water in a 2-quart pot on medium heat. Boil gently for 20 minutes and remove from heat. Garnish with green onion and sliced egg. Serve with table vinegar and pepper sauce.
Makes 4 servings

Hickory-Seasoned Mustard and Turnip Greens
(Low Sodium)

⅓ pound cured beef or pork

1 pound cleaned leafy mustard greens
1 1/4 pounds cleaned young turnip greens, with turnip
    roots
1/2 cup *each* chopped onions, red or green bell peppers,
    scallions
1 bay leaf
1/2 teaspoon *each* lemon pepper seasoning, ground
    cloves, onion powder, ground ginger, vegetable
    seasoning
2 tablespoons pure hickory liquid smoke

Parboil cured beef or pork for 40 minutes and rinse twice to remove salt. Wash and pick stems of mustard and turnip greens and cut 1-inch strip across leaves. Wash turnip roots. Cut off stem tops and root strings.

Combine all ingredients in 1 quart water in a 4-quart pot on high heat. Bring to a boil and reduce heat to medium. Cook 30 minutes covered, for vitamin retention or 60 minutes covered for southern-style tenderness. Serve immediately with hot corn bread and barbeque entree.

Makes 4 servings

Baked Cheddar Macaroni
(Low Sodium)

1 cube unsalted margarine
1/2 pound elbow macaroni
1/2 pound no- or low-sodium cheddar cheese, mild or
    sharp (two-thirds sliced 1/16 inch thick and cut in
    1/2-inch strips, one-third crumbled or diced)
1/2 cup finely chopped scallions
1/2 finely chopped onion-garlic
1/2 cup finely chopped celery
1/2 cup finely chopped red or green bell peppers
1 tablespoon blended seasoning (no salt, sugar, or MSG)
1 1/2 cups lowfat milk
1/2 teaspoon *each* onion powder, black pepper, ground
    cloves (from shakers)

Combine 1/4 cube margarine and 3 quarts water in a 6-quart pot. Bring to a boil on high heat. Stir in macaroni and reduce heat to medium. Boil for 15 minutes until three-fourths done and drain. To macaroni add crumbled or diced cheese, finely chopped vegetables, blended seasoning, 1/2 cup milk, and remaining ¾ cube margarine and mix thoroughly. From shakers, sprinkle on ½ teaspoon onion powder, black pepper, and ground cloves, or season to taste. Mix well.

Preheat oven to 350 degrees. Into a 2-inch-rimmed square or rectangular 2-quart baking dish pour half of mixed macaroni and spread evenly to form first layer. Evenly spread strips of cheese over macaroni. Spread remaining macaroni and top with rest of the cheese distributed evenly. Pour remaining cup of milk over macaroni and cover with aluminum foil, tightly sealing edges. Bake for 10 minutes. Uncover and bake until top begins to brown, about 5 minutes.

Makes 6 servings

 # Vegetable Brochettes with Cheese Sauce
(Low Sodium)

12 to 18 salad tomatoes
12 stemmed broccoli tops (about 1 pound)
12 to 18 small new potatoes (2 to 3 pounds) (or use 1½-
    to 2-inch pieces of cut potatoes with skins)
2 medium onions cut in 12 to 18 wedges
12 to 18 cherry peppers
1 zucchini sliced ½ to ¾ inch thick (dark green cucumber
    size)
Cheese sauce (recipe follows)

After all vegetables are washed and cut, place on 6 meat skewers, alternating 2 to 3 *each* of salad tomatoes, stemmed broccoli tops, potatoes, onion wedges, cherry peppers, and zucchini slices. Place brochettes 4 to 6 inches above pit fire for 7 to 10 minutes.

TO PREPARE CHEESE SAUCE
½ to ¾ pound low sodium jack or cheddar cheese
1½ cups lowfat or skim milk
½ cup chopped carrot
½ cup chopped green onions
½ teaspoon garlic parsley powder
½ teaspoon onion parsley powder
½ teaspoon black pepper
2 tablespoons red wine vinegar

Set cheese and milk aside. Combine and blender puree all other sauce ingredients (or finely grate carrots and mince green onions and mix with other ingredients). In a 2-quart pot on medium-high heat bring milk to a boil and reduce heat to medium low. Add vegetables and seasonings and simmer for 3 minutes. Remove from heat. When vegetable brochettes are done, add cheese to hot milk-vegetable blend, stirring thoroughly and melting cheeses on low heat for 1 minute. Remove from heat and serve sauce hot with skewered vegetables, spooning or pouring it over individual servings.

Makes 6 servings

Margarine-Fried Sweet Potatoes
(Salt Free)

Every time I prepare this dish, my craving for it goes back to a childhood memory when I was five years old and we would visit my mother's east Texas family settlement home on the farm in Jasper. While southern eating was always a treat, fried sweet potatoes served hot was a hit.

    1 to 1¼ pounds sweet potatoes, peeled and sliced ¼ inch
        thick
    1 teaspoon *each* cinnamon, nutmeg (from shakers)
    1 cube (4 ounces) unsalted margarine

Thoroughly wash sweet potatoes. Peel the potatoes and slice ¼ inch thick lengthwise, then cut them into pieces 2 to 3 inches long. Spread slices out and sprinkle very light coats of cinnamon and nutmeg on both sides.

Melt half of margarine in a 2-quart frying pan on medium heat until it becomes slightly hot. Place half of sliced sweet potatoes in pan in one layer. Fry, browning 3 to 4 minutes on each side, and remove from pan. Using second half of margarine, repeat the frying process for second half of sliced sweet potatoes.

Makes 4 to 6 servings

NOTE: If serving at cookout, place completely fried sweet potatoes in sizable aluminum throwaway pan. Just before barbeque meal is to be served, place on pit grill and warm over fire.

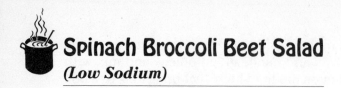

Spinach Broccoli Beet Salad
(Low Sodium)

1 or 2 cloves garlic (to rub salad bowl only)

²/₃ pound fresh crispy spinach, washed and torn into leafy
   bite-sized pieces

½ of 16-ounce can sliced beets (pickled if desired), slices
   cut in half (reserve beet juice)

½ pound chopped broccoli tops, thoroughly washed and
   cut into bite-sized pieces

⅓ pound low- or no salt jack cheese or milk, medium, or
   sharp cheddar cheese, diced

1 teaspoon no salt blended salad seasoning (or to taste)

1 to 2 cups unsalted croutons (optional)

Dressing Ingredients

½ teaspoon pure hickory liquid smoke

¼ cup finely chopped pimentos

3 tablespoons mayonnaise or prepared salad dressing

½ teaspoon low-salt regular or brown prepared mustard

1¼ cup pure vegetable oil

¼ cup red wine vinegar

¼ teaspoon *each* celery powder, onion parsley powder

2 tablespoons blended Italian herb salad seasoning

¼ cup beet juice (from 16-ounce can of beets)

TO PREPARE DRESSING

Combine all salad dressing ingredients in blender for ½ to 1 minute.

TO PREPARE SALAD

Thoroughly rub salad bowl with sliced garlic cloves and throw away used garlic pieces. Combine and loosely toss spinach, beets, broccoli and diced cheese in salad bowl. Add croutons if desired. Pour prepared dressing over tossed salad ingredients, toss again, and season to taste with no salt blended salad seasonings. Serve immediately.

Makes 4 hearty servings

Goobered* Fruit-Cottage Cheese Salad
(Sugarless)

2 medium-size apples, cored and diced
2 pears, cored and diced
1/4 pound fresh cherries, pitted
2 peaches, pitted and diced
1/4 pound seedless grapes
1 pound cottage cheese
1/4 pound chopped pecans, almonds or walnuts
Loose lettuce leaves

Combine fruit and nuts with cottage cheese and mix lightly. Serve on lettuce leaves.
Makes 6 servings

Fresh Fruit Coconut-Pecan Dessert
(Sugarless)

1 green eating apple, (unpeeled, cored, and diced)
3/4 basket strawberries, de-stemmed and halved (save 4 to
     6 whole or half berries for topping)
2 cups coarsely chopped fresh pineapple
1 large banana (half green ripe), peeled and sliced into
     1/4-inch pieces
1 cup unsalted pecans, crushed
1/2 of whole coconut (save coconut milk and very finely
     chop or grate coconut meat) or use 8-ounce package
     unsweetened coconut
juice of 1 lemon, seeded
1 can unsweetened whipped cream (for topping)

Combine apple, strawberries, pineapple, banana, and 1/2 cup of crushed pecans, and grated coconut with coconut milk (if used) and lemon juice. Mix lightly and divide among 4 cereal bowls or 6 dessert dishes. Top each

---

Generic African meaning for "nuts", not peanuts.

with desired amount of sugarless whipped cream, a strawberry, and a teaspoon of crushed pecans. Serve immediately or chill.

Makes 4 large, 6 small servings

Cheesy-Onion Wheat 'n' Cornmeal Muffins
(Low Sodium)

½ cup scallions (green onions), finely chopped
1 cup whole wheat flour, finely sifted
1 cup yellow cornmeal
1½ tablespoon baking powder
2 large or 3 small eggs
1 cup skim or lowfat milk
1 tablespoon vegetable oil (plus oil to grease pan)
¼ cube unsalted margarine, melted
1 cup (pressed in) grated cheddar cheese (or Swiss or
    jack if desired)

Preheat oven to 375 degrees. Grease 9-cup muffin pan with vegetable oil per muffin cup. In a 2-quart mixing bowl, combine whole wheat flour, cornmeal, baking powder, and onion powder. Thoroughly blend dry ingredients. Add eggs and milk. Mix and beat thoroughly for 1 minute until smooth. Add vegetable oil, melted margarine, scallions, and grated cheese desired. Beat and mix thoroughly. Pour even amounts of batter into each muffin cup. Bake for 20 minutes or until top is golden brown and springs back when lightly pressed.

Makes 9 muffins.

ABOUT THE AUTHOR

BOBBY SEALE, THE 1960S ACTIVIST AND VETERAN of the new left student protest era, was born in Dallas, Texas. He was raised by his carpenter father and Christian mother, and has been cooking and barbequing since he was twelve years old.

A man of many talents and skills, Bobby Seale has also been a stand-up comedian, actor, and jazz drummer. He learned carpentry at age five and grew up working in his father's building and furniture business in Oakland, California. During his four years enlistment in the U.S. Air Force, he was trained and worked as an aircraft sheet metal fabricator mechanic. Returning to Oakland in the early 1960's, Bobby Seale worked in the aerospace industry at night and during the day attended Merritt College as an engineering design major. With the advent of the Civil Rights Movement, he changed to the social sciences, influenced by Martin Luther King, Jr. and Malcolm X.

He co-founded the Black Panther Party (now defunct) in October 1966. During his eight years as chairman of the Black Panther Party, Bobby Seale was the key national co-ordinator/organizer, initiating community-based service programs such as breakfasts for school children, free busing for senior citizens, (SAFE — Seniors Against a Fearful Environment), preventative medical health care, co-operative housing, people's free food programs, and many others along with mass voter registration drives.

His international notoriety evolved most prominently during the 1969-70 Great Chicago Conspiracy Trial, depicted in the HBO T.V. docudrama written and directed by Jeremy Kagan, *Conspiracy: The Trial of the Chicago Eight*. Throughout all of his political trials (which he won *in the courtroom*), and his involvement with community services and political electorial organizing, Bobby Seale has kept barbequing.

Bobby Seale is currently a graduate student at Temple University pursuing a double major in political science and African-American studies. He is also assistant to Dean Lois S. Cronholm of the College of Arts and Science at Temple University, working with the program in social responsibility and with the minority recruitment committee for both undergraduate and graduate enrollment. His special emphasis is with minority recruitment for graduate work in the areas of physics, chemistry, biology, mathematics and engineering. Bobby Seale also volunteers as community liaison with Temple's Department of African-American Studies, and writing a second cookbook, plus two more works in the political sciences realm. He lectures extensively at other colleges and universities throughout the United States.

PUBLICATIONS BY BOBBY SEALE

1. *SEIZE THE TIME,* Random House, 1970, Hardcover and Vintage paper-back.

2. *A LONELY RAGE: THE AUTOBIOGRAPHY OF BOBBY SEALE* (Introduction by James Baldwin) - Times Books, 1978, Hardcover; Bantam Books, 1979, Paper.